Living Beyond Your Lifetime

Living Beyond Your Lifetime

How to Be Intentional about the Legacy You Leave

MIKE HUCKABEE

GOVERNOR OF ARKANSAS

BROADMAN
& HOLMAN
PUBLISHERS

Nashville, Tennessee

0–8054–2336–2

Published by Broadman & Holman Publishers,
Nashville, Tennessee

Unless otherwise noted, Scripture quotations are from the Holy Bible,
New International Version, copyright
© 1973, 1978, 1984 by International Bible Society.

Dewey Decimal Classification: 248
Subject Heading: CHRISTIAN LIFE

Library of Congress Cataloging-in-Publication Data

Huckabee, Mike, 1955–
    Living beyond your lifetime : how to be intentional about
the legacy you leave / Mike Huckabee.
        p.cm.
    ISBN 0–8054–2336–2
        1. Christian life—Baptist authors. I. Title.
    BV4501.2.H72 2000
    248.4'861—dc21

                                                        00–040409

1 2 3 4 5 04 03 02 01 00

Dedication

This book is dedicated to the memory of my parents, who gave me a legacy of believing that character and integrity are more valuable than wealth and that what we possess is less important than what kind of people we are.

Dorsey W. Huckabee, 1923–1996
Mae Elder Huckabee, 1925–1999

I further dedicate this book to the children of Arkansas. I genuinely hope to serve them so they will grow up healthier, better educated, and more responsible citizens who bring honor to themselves, their parents, and their God.

Contents

Foreword by Former President George Bush   ix

Acknowledgments   xi

Part I. A Legacy Lost

  1. Living Happily Ever After   3

  2. Potato Salad Time   11

  3. The Culture of the Moment   19

  4. The Politics of Personal Destruction   27

  5. Families in Free Fall   37

  6. From Love to Lust   47

Part II. A Legacy Learned

  7. Parents Do Matter   61

  8. The Faith Factor   71

  9. Faith with a Future: The Religion of Right On!   81

 10. Faith without a Future: The Religion of Right Now   91

 11. Winning an Election, Losing a Generation   95

 12. The Ditto Factor   105

Part III. A Legacy Lived

 13. The Power of Being Positive   115

 14. It's the Money, Honey   125

 15. Using What You Have   135

16. No Pain, No Gain   145

Part IV. A Legacy Loved

17. How Much Will You Leave Behind?   157
18. The Follow Factor   167
19. Toward the Exit Sign   177
20. The Legacy of Your Loot   193
21. Rare, Medium, or Well-Done?   203

"Keep Your Fork!"   209

Foreword

Governor Mike Huckabee, a true leader, writes about lasting legacies. This book effectively makes the point that service to others and thinking of generations to come is a lot of what life is all about.

There can be no definition of a successful life that does not include service to others, and Governor Huckabee in *Living Beyond Your Lifetime* drives home that point.

George Bush
Former President of the United States

Acknowledgments

This project has been a therapeutic experience for me, especially since my mother's death occurred between the time I started the book and the time I finished it. The encouragement from and patience of the wonderful editors and staff at Broadman & Holman, especially George W. Knight, John Landers, and Leonard G. Goss, kept me on track and kept me believing there was a message in all of this.

Dawn Cook, my personal assistant, sacrificed her time at night and on weekends to get the manuscript in order. Rex Nelson, my communications director by day, reverted to his old newspaper editor's habits at night to make sure things fit structurally and grammatically. There aren't many people to whom I would entrust such a task, but I never doubted my team.

My family has been most patient through this, and they've been willing to let me use most of my free moments late at night and on weekends to write the book. A special thanks to my wife, Janet, and my three children—John Mark, David and Sarah—along with my special pal, Jet, the First Dog, who sat at my

feet during the writing of every word and never complained, barked, or bit me. Maybe that's a good sign.

PART I

A Legacy Lost

ONE

Living Happily Ever After

"Once upon a time."

It was a nightly ritual for me as a child to hear a fairy tale that always started with the same words and always concluded with words that were anticipated for their satisfying sound. They marked the end of the story and let me know it was time to go to sleep.

You remember those words, don't you? I imagine a smile has already come to your face and the words have formed in your mind: "And they lived happily ever after."

As a child of the optimistic 1950s, I dreamed that life might be something like that. No matter what obstacles, dangers, and perils might come my way, in the end we could all "live happily ever after."

I was a teenager in the late 1960s. I was going to college and getting married in the 1970s. I was raising young children in the 1980s. I was raising teenagers in the 1990s. The journey has convinced me that while we all may start with certain expectations, life does not always lead to living happily ever after. Life is hard. It sometimes can be cruel, very cruel.

> *Life does not always lead to living happily ever after. Life is hard. It sometimes can be cruel, very cruel.*

One November day in 1984, just before Thanksgiving, I was asked to come to the local funeral home to bring comfort to a grieving family. No amount of seminary training could have prepared me for what was ahead. A day earlier, a young father in the process of a divorce picked up his two children, ages five and three, for what was to have been a trip to Wal-Mart to buy them a toy. The family was poor, so poor it had delayed an inevitable divorce. The mother kissed each of the children. She could not help but notice the joy in their eyes. They were filled with anticipation that the trip would yield a new toy.

After three or four hours, she became worried because they had not returned. She called the sheriff's office, and deputies started a search for the missing children. In the early afternoon of the following day, a deputy saw a car parked just off the highway. The vehicle fit the description of the car in which the children had last been seen. The officer parked his cruiser and began a search in the woods just beyond the car.

4

In a small clearing less than fifty yards from the edge of the highway, this veteran law enforcement officer saw something that would cause him to consider retirement and would forever mark the lives of all who would become involved in this situation. The father never took the children to Wal-Mart. He had purchased two nylon ski ropes and tied them together. He made slip knots that formed crude nooses and then tied the other end of the ropes to a limb just a few feet above the ground. With a child in each arm, he climbed a crudely constructed ladder. He placed the nooses around the necks of the children and then himself. He jumped, killing all three.

The children had attended Vacation Bible School the previous summer at the church where I was the pastor. It was apparently the only significant contact anyone in the family had with a church or a pastor. For that reason and because I was familiar with the staff at the funeral home, I was asked to come and bring some comfort to a hysterical mother.

Two of my children were almost the same ages as the two children who had been killed. I was now being asked to view the bodies of the dead children. As I escorted the mother to see them for the first time in their caskets, I thought about how unnatural the scene was. Here were what appeared to be sleeping little children with pudgy hands folded over, children who in their final moments on this earth surely must have asked, "Daddy, why are we here? Daddy, what is that rope for? Daddy, I don't want to get on that ladder. Daddy, this rope scratches my neck."

Compounding the horror was the report from the coroner, who indicated the children most likely did not die immediately and struggled to free themselves.

After the funeral service, Adam Robinson Jr., the funeral director with whom I had ridden to the cemetery, asked if I would like to stop for a cup of coffee. In the dozens of funeral services we had conducted together, we had never before made a stop on the way back. But today was different. I was glad he had mentioned it. I was no more ready to go back and face the normal routine than he was. We both needed some time for emotional reentry into a world that seemed cold and heartless.

It was the middle of the afternoon. We sat for an hour or so with very little conversation. We were oblivious to other customers in the small café and hardly aware of the coffee cups we held. Adam and I were close to the same age. We both had small children at home. Our children spent a little more time in our laps that evening and were hugged a little tighter.

Experiences like that take something out of you that is never replaced. You become aware that some things in life are not pretty and will never be OK. You realize that some of life's experiences will not have a fairy-tale ending. At such times it becomes more important than ever to begin assessing the difference between the immediate and the ultimate. What we do and how we live really do matter.

When we act on our passions of the moment and succumb to the feelings of "right now" without regard for the impact these actions will have, we have committed a grievous sin—letting our lifestyle ruin our lifetime.

I once was in an office with a sign that proclaimed, "Enjoy life. This is not a dress rehearsal."

How painfully true that is. Life is not a dress rehearsal. This is the real thing. We make choices that have consequences for a lifetime.

This book seeks to challenge the contemporary culture of "if it feels good, do it." Modern advertising bombards us with the message that life is all about me, it is all about now. Such messages may sell products and services, but they will cause us to sell our souls if we follow this philosophy to its logical conclusion.

> *Life is not a dress rehearsal. This is the real thing. We make choices that have consequences for a lifetime.*

Some events shake up the everyday routine, much like the agitator in the washing machine shakes loose the grime in our clothes. Such experiences are neither desired nor enjoyed. But they are necessary to force us to focus on the frailty of life and the certainty of death. They also force us to begin asking what really matters and why.

It is a safe bet that most of us will have passed from this life one hundred years from now. We have

7

no way of knowing if we have already celebrated our last birthday or observed our final Christmas. We will be challenged from time to time to ask whether in the final analysis our life really mattered and, if so, in what way and for whom. If we live, die, and that is all there is, then it may not matter a great deal what we do or how well we do it. But if we believe there is even a remote possibility that something about life matters because of the lasting implications our actions have, this should cause us to think differently, live differently, and leave a different kind of legacy.

> *More important than the money we are paid for our work is what we will become as a result of our work.*

Without apology, I believe the spiritual side of our lives really does matter. To believe otherwise is, in essence, to define persons as little more than animated protoplasm hopelessly going about our routines. I prefer to believe that as spiritual beings there is more to us than flesh and blood. If we do possess a soul capable of living beyond our lifetimes, then the seeds we plant in this life will yield fruit forever. If you believe those things, the ultimate becomes more important than the immediate.

Our responsibilities for the next generation will outweigh our roles in our current jobs. More important than the money we are paid for our work is what we will become as a result of our work. Our character will become more critical than the careers we follow.

For all of us, life began "once upon a time." Unlike the fairly tales, however, we are not assured that the last line of our life story will read, "And they lived happily ever after."

Questions for Reflection and Discussion

1. What experiences have you had that made you realize life is not always like a fairy tale—that we don't always "live happily ever after"?

2. What evidence do you see that our culture has accepted the dictum, "If it feels good, do it"?

3. In your opinion, what are some of the characteristics of a life that really matters? What are some of the characteristics of a life that counts for nothing?

4. What does the author mean by this statement: "As spiritual beings, there is more to us than flesh and blood"?

5. Why do you believe that what we do and how we live really do matter?

Potato Salad Time

I had never felt so alone in my life. I stood in a well-kept cemetery just off U.S. Highway 67 in Hope, Arkansas. I stared at the cold stone marker on which the names of my parents were etched along with the dates of their births and the dates of their deaths.

It's rare for me to be alone. I had asked the governor's security detail from the Arkansas State Police to give me some space. My mother had died on the last day of September 1999. On the horizontal plane, I have a sister and a wife. But vertically, for the first time, the only life links were descendants. When my mother drew her last breath, I had become the oldest living link my children had in their bloodlines on my side of the family.

The depth of my grief was not so much over the circumstances of my mother's death. Since a brain aneurysm and series of strokes in early 1992, her health had declined steadily. In her last days, it was no longer merciful to pray for continued existence as she was experiencing it. My unwavering faith that there was in fact a God in whose arms she would fall comforted me. I knew death was not the worst thing that could happen to her. Continuing in her state would, in fact, have been worse.

Some pain is far too intense to be expressed with the same emotions we once used for a scraped knee, a sad movie, or a loss in a championship basketball game.

It wasn't so much that she had died as it was the fact that her death had closed the book on an entire generation. Her passing had taken away my last link to the past and forever separated me from the one in whose womb I was formed.

It would have been easier if I could have shifted gears and wept bitterly. God has a wonderful way of washing away our grief with a cleansing shower of tears. But some pain is far too intense to be expressed with the same emotions we once used for a scraped knee, a sad movie, or a loss in a championship basketball game. I understood better Romans 8:26 (KJV): "Likewise the Spirit also helpeth our infirmities: for we know not what we should pray for as we ought: but the Spirit itself maketh intercession for us with groanings which cannot be uttered." The phrase "groanings which cannot be uttered" became more meaningful as I sought in the depth of my soul to find a vehicle of expression.

None of us got to choose how we came into this world. We can't choose our parents, our hometown, or the physician who ushers us into this life. Unless we were to end our life by our own hands, neither do we choose the circumstances or date of our death.

Even though we don't choose how we start life or how we end it, we most certainly choose how we live. It is how we live that may determine how people feel as they stand staring at our name chiseled into the gravestone. It is how we live that will affect generations to come and countless people whose names we don't even know.

In the South, there's a time-honored tradition that friends of the deceased bring more food to the family than can ever be eaten. After a loved one dies, there will soon be a parade of people, a pastor's visit, lots of hugs, and large bowls of potato salad. The potato salad is such a Southern fixture during the period of grief that some refer to it as "potato salad time."

"Potato salad time" is a good time to do some serious reflection about what really matters. No matter how busy we are, it's often in the presence of the potato salad that we're brought to a halt and reminded of how temporary this life is. Consuming large quantities of potato salad may not be good for your health, but being consumed by overwhelming doses of reality can be helpful.

You don't have to leave behind millions of dollars to have lived a life that matters. The size of your tombstone doesn't indicate the size of your life. I like to take casual walks through cemeteries and read the tombstones. You can learn a lot about a culture by spending time reading information on tombstones about the people whose voices are stilled but whose legacies live on. Most of their names never made the headlines. More died poor than rich in terms of money accumulated.

> *The real legacy of life cannot be calculated by an army of accountants. The value of one's life is seen in the character of those whose lives were touched.*

But many of the poorest in terms of material possessions died the richest because of the lives they lived and the legacies they passed on. The real legacy of life cannot be calculated by an army of accountants. The value of one's life is seen in the character of those whose lives were touched, be it children, extended family members, or even strangers who benefited in some way from a person's influence.

The theme of the popular Christmas movie *It's a Wonderful Life* comes to mind at "potato salad time."

As I wind through the part of life many know as midlife, I'm more acutely aware than ever that I'm on a collision course with the moment when that bowl of potato salad will be in memory of me.

I didn't grow up with wealth, but it was perhaps the lack of money that kept me from growing up always wanting more. I had the basics: food, shelter, clothing. Most of all, I had a family, a community, and a church. I realized I had all I really needed and more than I really deserved. As I continue the pilgrimage toward "potato salad time," I want to make sure I leave something behind that has far more value than money or property.

If my goal is not to leave behind a great deal of wealth, I'm succeeding wonderfully! Most of the really nice things I enjoy today are because of the job I do or the generosity of others. The lack of material wealth has been a blessing in many ways. Because it has not been my goal to own things, it has not been my life's curse to be owned by them. I can honestly say that deep within my soul I'm no happier living in a place known as "a mansion" (the governor's mansion in Little Rock) than I was when Janet and I occupied the north end of a forty-dollars-a-month duplex apartment.

In the following chapters, I hope you'll be challenged to think about living beyond your lifetime. I'm not referring to going to heaven and living the everlasting life by the resurrected power of Christ. Rather, I'm talking about living a life that will continue to be felt by those whose character wouldn't have been the same if the seeds of your faith and faithfulness had not been planted.

I remember vividly the first time I stood at the Tomb of the Unknown Soldier at Arlington National Cemetery in Arlington, Virginia. The soldier known only to God left not so much as his name, yet he was honored twenty-four hours a day, seven days a week. He represented our American freedom and its high cost. It's inconceivable to me that any American could stand at that place and not feel a sense of gratitude and pride.

I also have visited the great pyramids of Egypt twice and marveled at the extraordinary tombs of the ancient Egyptian pharaohs. While I was impressed with the architecture and innovation of the magnificent pyramids, I was struck with the thought that so much effort was made for the dead. You can't help but wonder if the effort might have been more productive had it been made for the living.

I've also visited the Jewish cemetery near Mount Zion in Jerusalem and stood at the grave of Oscar Schindler, who was immortalized in Stephen Spielberg's Oscar-winning film *Schindler's List*. Oscar Schindler failed at marriage and at business. He died poor, divorced, and lonely. But he had a legacy because when he had the opportunity, he acted to save the lives of others. Generations of Jewish families owe their existence to his courage and sacrifice.

Perhaps the most vivid memories come from my nine trips to Jerusalem and the realization there are two places vying for designation as the likely burial spot of Jesus Christ. The one thing both tombs have in common is that they are empty. But the thousands of visitors who flock to these sites each day to see that "he is not here, he has risen" (Mark 16:6) remind us of the most important legacy of all. That's the fact that this life, though important, is not the only one we live for. As we continue our pilgrimage, we will by faith share the legacy of our Lord in eternal life.

> *This life, though important, is not the only one we live for. As we continue our pilgrimage, we will by faith share the legacy of our Lord in eternal life.*

Still, it's important to live as though this life really matters. The seeds we plant will bear fruit through the character of those who live beyond us and our "potato salad time."

Questions for Reflection and Discussion

1. What's the difference between owning things and being owned by things?

2. What legacy have people like Oscar Schindler left the world?

17

3. What legacy have your parents left you? What type of legacy are you working to leave your children?

4. What legacy has Jesus Christ left the Christian believer?

5. Which is more important—a material legacy or a spiritual legacy? Why?

THREE

The Culture of the Moment

Dick Morris sat on the edge of his bed in the small, crowded room on the sixth floor of the Camelot Hotel in downtown Little Rock. It was 8:30 P.M. on July 29, 1993, and the polls had been closed for less than an hour after a special election for the office of lieutenant governor. This was the only item on the ballot in Arkansas that day.

Ordinarily an election for lieutenant governor would draw little media attention. But this race was different. The office was vacant because Arkansas' former governor, Bill Clinton, had been sworn in as president and the lieutenant governor, Jim Guy Tucker, had moved up to governor.

The vacancy for lieutenant governor was in the political spotlight during the summer of 1993. The race had become much more than a contest for the office itself. This was the first major election in Arkansas following Clinton's move to the White

House. Up to that point in 1993, Republicans had put together a clean sweep of major elections. Later that year, governor's races in New Jersey and Virginia would be claimed by the GOP.

On this sultry day, political eyes nationwide were focused on Arkansas to see what would happen in the new president's backyard. Morris was no stranger to Arkansas political races or to conducting political polls to determine how those races were going. He had worked for Clinton in every one of the president's political races except his unsuccessful 1974 race for Congress and his unsuccessful 1980 race for governor.

Only a handful of results came in during the first hour after the polls closed at 7:30 P.M. As each new total was posted, Morris would scratch furiously on a yellow legal pad and then enter the figures in a pocket calculator. Just past 8:30 P.M. with less than 15 percent of the precincts having reported, Morris turned to me and in a matter-of-fact tone of voice said, "Congratulations, you're going to be elected lieutenant governor with 51 percent of the vote."

It would be another ninety minutes before the rest of the ballots were counted and the results were clear enough for my opponent to concede and for me to walk on the stage and face a cheering crowd of supporters. I declared victory with 51 percent of the vote. How could he possibly have known the outcome so much earlier with so little information?

That night, I began recognizing the power of scientific polling to recognize trends, attitudes, and movement of public opinion. In today's politics, having a competent pollster can be expensive but not nearly as expensive as not having the information the pollster can generate. Good information ensures that the right campaign decisions are made.

During subsequent campaigns, I have come to appreciate even more the value of public opinion research. Dick Dresner has been my pollster since 1996 and has proven invaluable to me. He helps make sure the campaign message is having the desired impact on the voters.

Polling is much like using a thermometer. A thermometer can read the temperature and give an accurate assessment of where things stand at a given moment. What polling cannot do, however, is serve as a thermostat capable of not only reading the temperature but adjusting it and making it what it should be.

> *For a candidate to express a belief only because it reflects public sentiment is not what a republican form of government is about.*

It is important for a political candidate to know what the public believes. But for a candidate to express a belief only because it reflects public sentiment is not what a republican form of government is about. A pressing need of our culture is people whose lives are built upon clear, carefully considered principles. Too many people are being led by those who make decisions based only on what people claim to want rather than what is right or wrong.

As a teenager in my hometown of Hope, Arkansas, I often would hear my pastor say, "If you don't stand for something, you will fall for anything." Corporate leaders, political leaders, church leaders, and families are at their best when they are motivated by principles rather than public opinion.

> *Law is the imperative of love. The essence of the Ten Commandments is to depict what love looks like.*

What are some principles worth living by? Ask a roomful of people, and you possibly will get a roomful of answers. But there already exists a code of principles established thousands of years ago and adhered to by people from a variety of religious backgrounds. It has been accepted as a basis for appropriate behavior. Fortunately, no one has copyrighted the Ten Commandments.

Although some attempts have been made to prohibit these principles from being displayed, they have survived through the ages. They are the foundation for most of our laws and commonly accepted codes of human behavior.

Law always reveals the character of the people who created it. Therefore, God's law reveals the character of a God who delivered it. In the Ten

Commandments, law is the track on which the train of love rides. Law is the imperative of love. The essence of the Ten Commandments is to depict what love looks like.

The Ten Commandments are divided into two sections—the vertical laws dealing with man's relationship with God and the horizontal laws dealing with man's relationship with others. Jesus would say the entire law could be summed up in two basic principles: To love God with all of your heart and to love your neighbor as yourself. This essentially captures our responsibility to God and others.

Some people have attempted to portray the "thou shalt not" of the law to be essentially negative. Understood in the proper context, however, these commandments are positive affirmations of life-giving, legacy-building principles.

Here is a look at the basic laws that appear in Exodus 20:1–17:

1. *You shall have no other gods before me.* This is an affirmation that God can be known in such a way as to create a relationship strong enough to dismiss the need for further searching.

2. *You shall not make for yourself an idol.* The Creator God cannot be confined to a tangible object that can be sold, lost, or destroyed. A god who is visible is a god who is definable and therefore limited to the form in which it exists. The true God cannot be confined. He refuses to conform to our culture.

3. *You shall not misuse the name of the Lord your God.* This principle affirms that God's name should not be used carelessly. One must not treat his love with contempt.

4. *Remember the Sabbath day by keeping it holy.* True love makes special time for those who are loved. The principle behind a day of rest was not to have a day when we forget God but a day when we remember him.

> *Real love respects authority. A person must learn to cope with authority first in the home.*

5. *Honor your father and your mother.* Real love respects authority. A person must learn to cope with authority first in the home.

6. *You shall not murder.* This commandment is an affirmation of the sacredness of human life and a reminder that the real goal of love is always to heal, not to hurt.

7. *You shall not commit adultery.* The devastation of adultery is that it defrauds the love of another and destroys the self-esteem of the one being defrauded. Promises and vows are sacred, and the seventh commandment affirms the validity and authority of such promises.

8. *You shall not steal.* True love has the desire to give instead of take.

9. *You shall not give false testimony against your neighbor.* Gossip and outright falsehoods defy the character of a God who is always honest. Love is always honest. Dr. Vester Wobler was for many years chairman of the department of religion at my alma mater, Ouachita Baptist University in Arkadelphia, Arkansas. I still recall his wise advice to his freshmen students. He admonished us to tell the truth and nothing but the truth but never to be so dumb that we told all the truth we knew. Some seek to justify the spreading of rumors in the name of concern or even correction. But each of us should be careful to speak well of others.

> *A person who has no standard to live by other than the culture of the moment is a person whose principles might as well come from the latest public opinion polls.*

10. *You shall not covet.* Love delights in the possessions of others rather than desiring what others have and feeling jealous about what they have.

The law reveals God's depth of character, and it also reveals our lack of character. Laws are a giant mirror reflecting not only what is but projecting what ought to be, giving us the standard against which to compare our lives.

A person who has no standard to live by other than the culture of the moment is a person whose principles might as well come from the latest public opinion polls. This would be like repairing an appliance by holding it against a mirror rather than reading the directions to determine how it should be performing.

Questions for Reflection and Discussion

1. Why does our culture need people whose lives are built upon clear, carefully considered principles?

2. What do the Ten Commandments tell us about the character of God?

3. Which of the Ten Commandments are most important—those that deal with our relationship to God or those that deal with our relationship to others?

4. Why is the commandment to "honor your father and your mother" so vitally important?

5. Can you recall a specific instance when a government official made a decision based on principle rather than public opinion?

6. Why are the promises and vows that we make to others important to God?

FOUR

The Politics of Personal Destruction

President Clinton coined the phrase "politics of personal destruction" during the Whitewater scandal and the subsequent impeachment process. Although he admitted he had lied to a grand jury, the president managed to avoid ouster from office. He did so by appealing to the growing distaste of Americans for a political system in which candidates are portrayed as bad people rather than a system in which competing ideas are debated.

Elective politics is not the only realm in which there is character assassination. It can be the politics of the business office or even the politics of the church. It also can be true of marriage and the family. Many people determine it is better to divorce their partners than to work to develop a deeper intimacy.

Even by the standards of Jesus, it is not wrong to have enemies. But it is wrong to hate them. Jesus had enemies. Most of us find it inevitable as we go

> *Even by the standards of Jesus, it is not wrong to have enemies. But it is wrong to hate them.*

through life that we will encounter people who are considered enemies. President Lincoln said that we should love our enemies because they are the only ones who will always tell us the truth.

It is easy to love our friends. But loving our enemies requires an extraordinary touch of grace and a true understanding of what love means. Loving our enemies does not mean giving in to their demands or compromising our values. None of us have the capacity to control the actions of others. But we are responsible for our reactions to the behavior of others.

One of the most misunderstood admonitions of the Bible is the instruction on dealing with bad behavior that is directed toward us. The ancient code of retaliation known as "an eye for an eye" (Exod. 21:24) is actually a marked improvement over the more barbaric attitude, "Cut out my eye and I will cut off your head."

Most of our hearts are ruled more by a sense of revenge than a sense of justice. Revenge is a drive that is natural to us. We want more than just getting even. Jesus cited three examples of unfair actions that we might encounter. If we are struck on the right cheek, we are to turn the other cheek. If we are sued for our coat, we are admonished to give it up voluntarily. And if we are forced to do a duty that we don't want to do, we are encouraged to go the "second mile"—to do more than required (see Matt. 5:39–42).

In the ancient culture in which Jesus lived, a strike on the right cheek was an insulting blow to a person's dignity and pride. The coat represented people's legitimate possessions, which were necessary for covering and warmth. And the first mile a person was compelled to travel was his or her duty under the Roman legal code.

Jesus set new standards by telling us we should never be content to do only what is expected of us. We should go to the next level by living and giving beyond our obligations and expectations. The way to win over an enemy is not to conquer but to serve. When a person goes beyond the expected duties and responsibilities, he or she demonstrates higher qualities of excellence, leadership, and accomplishment.

Getting ahead today often means disabling others so they are unable to complete the race. But such an approach does not represent getting ahead at all. There is no honor in such a victory—only shame. When the associates and husband of former Olympic skater Tonya Harding were accused of attacking competitor Nancy Kerrigan, the world was repulsed. Without able and honorable competition, victory in any endeavor is meaningless.

The restaurant that eliminates a competitor across the street by starting a whispering campaign about

> *Jesus set new standards by telling us we should never be content to do only what is expected of us. We should go to the next level by living and giving beyond our obligations and expectations.*

people getting food poisoning at that eatery might succeed for a time. Ultimately, though, quality and service of the surviving restaurant will decline without competition.

Loving others is not the same as performing according to the demands of others. We do not truly love an alcoholic by giving him what he craves—another drink. True love must draw the line and say no. Genuinely caring about another person does not necessarily mean doing what that person demands. By the same token, eliminating competition is not nearly as productive in the long term as besting the competition.

A basketball team that never plays a game but advances due to the forfeiture of other teams is not prepared to play its best. A politician who seeks to win an election by destroying the reputation of his opponents will eventually die by the sword.

Living life for the ultimate—living beyond our lifetime—requires that we think not in terms of getting rid of those who oppose us. Instead, we should overcome them with superior ideas and values. The most effective way to prove that one car is better than another on the track is not to let the air out of the tires of the competition.

People whose principles are well grounded are not afraid of competition. Elijah challenged the prophets of Baal on Mount Carmel. After inviting them to call upon their god to consume a sacrifice on the altar, he called upon God to do the same (1 Kings 18:20–39). It is a big mistake for people of integrity and faith to believe that they advance their cause by destroying the competition.

> *A politician who seeks to win an election by destroying the reputation of his opponents will eventually die by the sword.*

If you believe your faith leads to God, then let others see God's qualities in you. Do you believe your business offers the best products at the best prices? Then let satisfied customers become your unofficial and most effective sales force. Do you believe your candidate is the best for the job and would serve most effectively? Then push the platform of that candidate rather than attacking opponents.

When promises made become promises kept, the public will have confidence. It has been my experience that people are more willing to accept a candidate whose acts are consistent with his stated convictions than one who spouts the popular view but never succeeds in translating that view into positive results.

General Robert E. Lee was once asked to give his opinion of a man who had spoken ill of him on many occasions. Lee spoke kindly of the man. One of his aides could stand it no longer and spoke up. "General, you have spoken very kindly of this individual, but he has taken every opportunity to speak hatefully about you," he said. "Why would you say such nice things about him?"

> *The challenge of living beyond our lifetime begins with being more than a critic of what is wrong. We must strive to be a creator of what is right.*

Lee replied, "I was asked my opinion of him, not his opinion of me."

We need more people who can engage in issues of importance while remaining on the high road, avoiding the ditches of personal destruction. Some wag observed that contemporary politics is like a demolition derby and that whoever is still standing at the finish line will be the winner. For the sake of public civility, we must convince people that winning ultimately is more important than winning immediately.

Not only is it inevitable to have enemies; it may be desirable. Enemies can provide the necessary

32

traction for one's principles. They help us learn perseverance and teach us to love people who are not very lovable. The challenge of living beyond our lifetime begins with being more than a critic of what is wrong. We must strive to be a creator of what is right.

The people who scream "kill the umpire" tend to be those who are sitting in the cheapest seats in the park. I am amused whenever I listen to sports talk shows on the radio. It is apparent that people who have never played a down of football are capable of giving a detailed analysis of what is wrong with the team and comment on how various players have failed to perform adequately. These are people whose qualifications consist of watching sports on television while consuming their weight in potato chips and beer. Truly successful people are more critical of themselves than they are of others.

> *Although attacking others will sometimes work with voters, it will not work as we stand before God's judgment seat. He will judge based on what he knows, not on what our critics have said about us.*

I have become increasingly amused by editorial writers and self-appointed political reformers who think they know how to solve all the problems faced by the government. They are not subject to the levels of disclosure they demand of elected officials. They have never had to implement decisions in the complex world of partisan politics—a world that is open to public scrutiny.

My family has had to endure attacks I never would have imagined before running for office. Frivolous lawsuits instigated by political opponents who are unable to find real issues can create distractions from the tasks at hand. Some members of the media are willing to take baseless allegations and not only report them but repeat them over and over.

Although attacking others will sometimes work with voters, it will not work as we stand before God's judgment seat. He will judge based on what he knows, not on what our critics have said about us.

Questions for Reflection and Discussion

1. Do you agree with this statement by the author: "Genuinely caring about another person does not necessarily mean doing what that person demands"? Why or why not?

2. How does God's judgment of us differ from the human judgments that most of us have to endure?

3. In your opinion, why did Jesus exhort us to love our enemies?

4. What was the ancient code of retaliation known as "an eye for an eye"?

5. According to the author, contemporary politics is like a "demolition derby." Do you agree or disagree with this assessment? What evidence of this "demolition derby" approach have you observed in recent political campaigns?

FIVE

Families in Free Fall

The young minister stood before a large congregation, performing the first wedding ceremony of his career. Not even the bride was as nervous as the newly ordained pastor. He feared butchering a high-dollar wedding involving one of the church's most influential families.

Soon, his anxiety turned to sheer terror. Having seated the audience, he opened his Bible, only to realize he had forgotten to place the notes to the wedding ceremony in the Bible. He thought he could recite the ceremony by memory, but to calm himself he decided to begin by quoting some Scripture.

Unfortunately, as he stood facing the bride and groom and hundreds of waiting guests, the Scripture that came to his mind and out of his month was, "Father, forgive them; for they know not what they do."

The young minister was probably more right than wrong in his assessment of the situation before him. Our culture is failing in its understanding of the proper role of marriage. About half of the marriages performed in the United States will end in divorce. Little seems to be learned from the first marriage since the likelihood of divorce increases sharply in second and third marriages.

> *The cost to society for failed marriages is too high to calculate. In most instances, only the lawyers come out winners.*

Until recently, my own state of Arkansas had the second-highest divorce rate in the nation. Only Nevada had a higher divorce rate than Arkansas. Fortunately, these numbers have changed somewhat. I have challenged the people of my state to reduce the divorce rate by half during the next decade by declaring a state of marital emergency. We have encouraged pastors in each city to adopt community marriage policies in which couples are required to have premarital counseling.

Why does it matter? While there are many wonderful exceptions for which we can be grateful, the overwhelming statistical evidence points out that divorce dramatically increases the likelihood of poverty. Children growing up without the benefit of two parents are more likely to get involved in drugs, alcohol, premarital sex, juvenile delinquency, and academic failure. The cost to society for failed marriages is too high to calculate. In most instances, only the lawyers come out winners.

One of the reasons so many marriages fail is that couples have accepted the myth that the purpose of marriage is to be happy. If the expectations for a marriage arise from a sentimental love story filled with constant excitement, adventure, and romance, the couple is headed for disappointment. The shocking reality is that marriage represents a cultural collision. Two independent individuals who have lived under different rules, habits, and lifestyles suddenly join together in a relationship designed to be a lifelong laboratory of learning how to love.

I remember years ago telling a young couple during counseling that God's primary goal for their marriage was not necessarily for them to be happy. The groom interrupted and said, "Well, that is good to hear. Apparently we are succeeding."

If the goal of marriage is not to be happy, then what is it?

The word *happiness* is derived from "happenstance," suggesting that pleasure is derived from external conditions that are subject to change without our being able to control them. According to this definition, happiness is based on how we feel and what kinds of conditions surround us—whether we have good health, plenty of money, friends who support us, and an absence of conflict, illness, and unexpected calamity.

Few people live in a world of unbroken pleasure. Most of us live in an imperfect world. The toast is burned. Our car battery is dead. The traffic on the

> *The purpose of marriage is to establish a relationship in which we learn to love another person in the sacrificial and unselfish manner that God loves us. Marriage allows us to develop the character traits of patience and kindness.*

way to work is horrible. Other drivers are rude. The boss is mean. We get notice of an IRS audit. The dog chews up our favorite shoes. The long-anticipated football game is interrupted by an outage of the cable system.

Since the first wedding was performed by God and since he authored life and the instructions on how to live it, we need to discover exactly what the instructions are for marriage before we seek to live it.

When my oldest son was three years old, I attempted to put together a tricycle for him the night before Christmas. I confess to having the mechanical aptitude of a bull. After hours of frustration and hard work, I completed the task of putting together the tricycle shortly after 2:00 A.M. I was fortunate to be able to assemble the tricycle. But why did the manufacturer include more parts than I found necessary to complete the task?

The tricycle tipped slightly to the right and had a rear wheel that did not turn as easily as the others, but I had completed the task. During the two years my son rode that tricycle, I always wondered how it might have turned out if I had read the instructions.

Many couples spend dozens of hours and their parents spend thousands of dollars preparing for a wedding that will last maybe twenty minutes. On the other hand, they spend little time and virtually no money preparing for marriage, which is supposed to last a lifetime. Is it any wonder that in our culture many families are in free fall?

By saying the purpose of marriage is not to be happy, I'm not suggesting the primary goal of marriage is misery. The purpose of marriage is to establish a relationship in which we learn to love another person in the sacrificial and unselfish manner that God loves us. Marriage allows us to develop the character traits of patience and kindness. These are not natural to our selfish nature, but they are quite natural to God's nature.

Marriage is a way to discover our own worth through sacrificial service. Those who search for happiness often believe that changing circumstances will change their condition—a better job, a better house, a better car, and a better spouse are the elements that will make one "happy." Those who are always looking to change the circumstances are likely to end up in one of two conditions—(1) resentful for never having achieved that elusive sense of what it means to be happy, or (2) resigned to a life in which they feel trapped in emotional pain or abuse.

One of the most significant reasons for the failure of marriages is that couples focus on how they expect to feel in the next thirty minutes rather than what they expect to be in the next thirty years. God's view of marriage is not based on the condition of being satisfied by one's partner. Couples should focus on serving each other and finding satisfaction in fulfilling each other.

When many couples say "I love you," what they really mean is, "I love me and am willing to use you as a vehicle for my expression of self-love." To understand how we are to love, we need to look not in the mirror but toward heaven. We are to discern how God loves us.

God does not love us because we are lovable. He does not love us because we meet certain conditions—such as giving a specific amount to charity, attending church, or even being polite. He loves us because it is his nature and his choice to love us. He loves us without regard for whether we are worthy, will return his love, or even acknowledge his existence.

No matter how good we are, God could love us no more. And no matter how bad we are, he could love us no less. His love is prompted by nothing we do. It comes from his own character.

We are not born with an aptitude for sacrificial, selfless love. We are born with the desire to put ourselves first. Human nature drives us to see to it that our own needs are met. Sin is spelled with a small *s* and a small *n* with a big *I* in the middle.

Even when we pretend to be humble, there are those moments in which our true nature bursts forth. Have you been part of a group photograph recently? When you had a chance to look at it, whose image did you glance at first? Did you judge how good the photo was based on how you looked?

When marriage is based on how we feel about each other, we are headed for disaster. Marriage should be based not on our emotions and how we feel but on our devotion and what we choose to do in seeking the best for our partner. Marriages fail for the same reason that people fail. They are overwhelmed with selfishness. One of the great promises of the Bible is that God will never leave us or forsake us. Many marriages are based on the premise that if you don't perform up to my expectations, I will leave you and forsake you.

None of us stand at the marriage altar and expect our marriage to fail. Divorce is the unnatural conclusion to a relationship that started with wonderful expectations and ended with deep hurt and shattered

> *No matter how good we are, God could love us no more. And no matter how bad we are, he could love us no less. His love is prompted by nothing we do. It comes from his own character.*

hopes. But no amount of prayer or patience can hold a marriage together when one of the partners is determined to destroy it.

Every married couple should understand that marriage was designed to last a lifetime. Marriage should teach us how to love. Marriage is more than a temporary lifestyle in which we use another person in order to meet our own needs.

Some wag said that a man's life consists of twenty years of his mother asking where he is going, forty years of his wife asking where he has been, and one hour (at his funeral) with everyone wondering where he ended up. The basis for a successful marriage is not that two people learn to be independent. Rather, they should choose to relinquish their independence for the purpose of building a relationship of interdependence. A marriage in which the two partners don't actually need each other is a marriage that has already failed.

> *Marriages fail for the same reason that people fail. They are overwhelmed with selfishness.*

It is the nature of a husband to want to be wanted. A man is motivated if he believes his wife truly needs and wants him. A wife must have similar feelings about her husband. When a couple does not share a mutual need for each other, they are headed toward disaster.

44

One of the tragedies of a failed marriage is that it creates a model for children. A failed marriage sends the message to children that marriage is temporary rather than forever. It promises commitments to vows on the front end. But the reality is that those vows matter only as long as someone feels comfortable in keeping them. The message that divorce sends to children is that if you do not get what you want out of a relationship, it is permissible to abandon it and seek the fulfillment of your desires somewhere else.

> *A marriage in which the two partners don't actually need each other is a marriage that has already failed.*

Is it any wonder that many children of divorce have a heightened sense of insecurity and a lack of trust? The people closest to them, the very people responsible for teaching them how to love, walk off before the job is complete. How can we expect anything other than a generation of children who believe promises are made to be broken? They learn that vows are nothing more than intentions that reside within the boundaries of ever-changing emotions.

We have made a mess of marriage by failing to understand that its purpose is to build a lifelong legacy.

Questions for Reflection and Discussion

1. In your opinion, why is the divorce rate so high in our contemporary culture?

2. In what sense does marriage represent a "cultural collision," according to the author? Do you find this true in your own marriage?

3. Why do many children whose parents were divorced have a heightened sense of insecurity and a lack of trust?

4. In your opinion, what are some things couples can do to prepare more adequately for marriage? How can the church assist couples in making this preparation?

5. Do you agree with this statement by the author: "Marriage should be based not on our emotions and how we feel but on our devotion and what we choose to do in seeking the best for our partner"? Why or why not?

From Love to Lust

The director of family policy for the governor's office told me a group of women wanted him to attend a news conference denouncing a major retailer's catalog because of offensive photos and text. My first reaction was to roll my eyes and imagine a bunch of well-meaning but sheltered women who had stumbled across the latest edition of a lingerie catalog.

He recognized my reluctance and said, "Before you decide, take a look at the material they are talking about."

As I thumbed through two catalogs and other promotional materials from a popular retailer that caters to teenagers, I was taken aback. I knew it as a store that targets kids like my daughter and many of her peers. I was stunned to see a mainline national retailer publish what they deemed a "catalog" with occasional references to their merchandise mixed with stories of a pedophile whose job as a department store Santa

Claus gave him the opportunity to delight in little girls bouncing on his lap.

There also were stories of a pornographic movie queen complete with nude photos of her and her graphic descriptions of a sex life that almost begged for sexually transmitted diseases. There was graphic frontal nudity. Most of the females captured in the nude appeared to be young teenagers, often in the embrace of males who looked to be in their thirties.

The company asserted that all of the women photographed were older than eighteen. In comparison to some of the pornographic magazines on the newsstand, this catalog could indeed be considered tame. But it was repulsive that such a publication was being used to market trendy clothing to teenagers. One television commentator discussing the resulting publicity furor remarked how ironic it was for a company to try to sell clothing by picturing people who did not have any.

The company defended the publication, saying that it came in a plastic wrap with a warning sticker. Obviously, they said, it was intended for adults. If that defense were valid, cigarette smoking would have ended in this country three decades ago based on the warning labels printed on each pack.

I do not call for our government to determine what people can or can't believe or what they can or can't see. As governor, I had no power to order such marketing ploys off the shelves. However, my role as a parent caused me to explain to my daughter why my money would no longer be used to buy clothing for her at that store.

If we are to leave a legacy for the next generation, we need to understand what kind of legacy we are losing as a result of confusing lust with love. There is something tragic about a culture that loses the capacity to express sacrificial love for another. We have abandoned that idea in exchange for ego-centered love that uses other people as vehicles for our personal satisfaction.

Defenders of pornography point to the U.S. Constitution. Indeed, the First Amendment protects material that is merely offensive. But repeated U.S. Supreme Court decisions have affirmed that obscenity is not protected free speech. Even if the Constitution did allow for child pornography, bestiality, and female mutilation, for people of faith there is a document more binding than the Constitution and more clear in its understanding of what is right and wrong.

> *There is something tragic about a culture that loses the capacity to express sacrificial love for another. We have abandoned that idea in exchange for ego-centered love that uses other people as vehicles for our personal satisfaction.*

We trade a legacy of love for a legacy of lust in this sensuality-saturated society in at least five ways.

Attack Against Morality

To some people's surprise, I'm not nearly the prude my critics portray me to be. Nudity in art and the movies is not automatically offensive to me. I don't use profanity or tolerate it in my office. However, I recognize it is a part of our culture and accept it as part of the language we must live with. It is not the presence of such things that are offensive. It is the context in which they are presented that moves them from expression to excess. Too often, nudity and profanity are used so a weak idea can receive strong attention.

> *Too often, nudity and profanity are used so a weak idea can receive strong attention.*

Society's view of sensuality has changed dramatically since Hugh Hefner came out with the first edition of *Playboy* magazine. Who would have thought that a generation later what was then a scandalous adult magazine would be milder than a catalog published by a retailer trying to attract business from teenagers?

As we pass the generational torch, perhaps we should ask if we are better off as a nation because of these changes. Are families stronger? Are schools safer? Are incest, rape, and child molestation less prevalent today? Do our children have more respect for teachers, God, and government? Are people more content with themselves and their marriages?

If we are a better nation, why do drug dogs patrol our school campuses? Why do we find it necessary to build rape crisis centers? Why must our police officers wear bulletproof vests as part of their standard equipment? Why are more psychiatric hospitals being built, even in small communities?

No one would suggest that obscene materials are the sole cause of the deterioration of our morals. A strong argument can be made that private morals are private and not the domain of government. But a stronger argument can be made that the public has the right to determine what is in the best interest of all citizens.

We regulate liquor sales and used car dealers. We make sure the kitchens in restaurants are clean. Even if I don't eat in a certain restaurant, my taxes help pay to have it inspected. When sex crimes are committed, my tax dollars must be used to pay the court costs, the prison costs, the social service costs. The issue moves from private morality to public morality.

Citizens do, in fact, have the right to determine what we consider appropriate as a society. It has become a cliché to shout, "You can't legislate morality!" But this is a contradictory statement. All legislation determines the morality of an issue. It would be correct to say that you cannot legislate behavior. But every law sets a standard for society.

The speeding laws determine what is wrong when it comes to how fast you drive. Laws prohibiting murder define the morality of killing. No one can force another person to believe the same things he does. But self-governing people have the right to place boundaries on what can be bought and sold, whether it is heroin, a prostitute's body, or videos that depict adults having sex with children.

Attack Against the Mind

University studies from the United States and Canada confirm that pornography is addictive. Most people move from mild to more bizarre forms of pornography over time. In the more extreme cases, movies about sex with animals and with children are marketed to those who no longer are titillated by an air-brushed photo of a topless twenty-year-old.

The day before his execution for multiple murders, rapes, and sexual torture of women and children, Ted Bundy confessed that the pornography he saw as a child fed his obsession for more until he progressed to a state of total depravity. Counselors can attest to the fact that there are indeed "pornoholics." Unlike those who sneak an occasional peek at sexually explicit material, these people are increasingly addicted to more explicit versions of smut.

Attack Against Marriage

A man who will gaze at an electronically enhanced photo of a model in a magazine will tend to view his wife with increasing disrespect. The reality she projects contrasts sharply with the fantasy of the magazine page or the video screen. It should come as no surprise that the needs of many wives go unmet because their husbands are trying to meet their needs through a sexual encounter with a photograph. These men seek to satisfy their sexual needs with photographs of women they don't know, while the wives they have promised to cherish are neglected.

Attack Against Motherhood

Sex for trade is an affront to the values we need in the mothers who raise America's children. Would anyone suggest that a child be raised by a prostitute who has been with men who paid for her services by the hour? Would anyone suggest it is a nurturing environment for a child to have a mother who is sleeping with a different man every night—a mother who would subject herself to savage treatment by strange men again and again? Do we want children growing up believing a woman's value is based on her external beauty while denying the existence of inner beauty and character?

Attack Against Manhood

Sexually explicit materials perpetuate the myth that a "real man" is one who treats women with savage selfishness. Pornography encourages man to have no regard for the person his sexual partner really is but to view a woman as a plaything to be discarded when "it" no longer brings him pleasure. This furthers the lie that sex is primarily biological. We forget the spiritual and emotional dimensions that were intended when sex was designed by God. The modern view of sex reduces one's highest worth to a bodily function and forsakes the meaning of honor, character, and consideration for others.

The modern view of sex reduces one's highest worth to a bodily function and forsakes the meaning of honor, character, and consideration for others.

I have yet to meet a man who wants his son to grow up and become a customer of prostitutes. I have never had a man say to me that his goal was for his son never to experience a date with a decent girl or enjoy a lifetime with a decent family. I have yet to meet a man who dreams that his daughter will be a centerfold model, with strange eyes leering lustfully at her image. It is inconceivable that any father would want his daughter to be the object of thousands of male strangers who imagine themselves in bed with her.

There is a point at which feminists and most conservatives agree. They agree it is disgusting to treat women as things and not respect the personhood of women. Every human being deserves to be treated with dignity and respect. An individual should never be considered as another person's property. I cannot imagine that any sane person would argue that we return to a system of slavery. But pornography does just that. It enslaves the predator in a downward spiral of lust and seeks to make a slave of those who are the objects of lustful desire.

Why is it necessary to deal with such a topic as we look toward our legacy? Let's hope it is because we have tired as a society of seeing tears flowing down the faces of wives whose husbands have come to love the pages of a magazine more than their spouses. I hope we have grown tired of hearing five- and six-year-old children tell of molestation by parents. I hope it is because we have tired of seeing the devastation of women who are promised love but given lust by hormone-driven adolescents who are ready to toss aside one person they treated as a toy in pursuit of yet another.

> *I cannot imagine that any sane person would argue that we return to a system of slavery. But pornography does just that. It enslaves the predator in a downward spiral of lust and seeks to make a slave of those who are the objects of lustful desire.*

What about our freedom? Do we have the right to do as we please?

- We are free to drive, but the law restricts our speed, which direction we travel, and whether we wear seat belts.

- We are free to be filthy, but we are not free to walk into a hospital operating room in that condition.

- We are free to vote, but we are not free to vote on someone else's ballot or vote more than once.

- We are free to express an opinion, but we are not free to place a loudspeaker in a neighborhood at 2:00 A.M.

- We are free to worship, but we are not free to sit down in a busy intersection to pray, backing up traffic for miles.

- We are free to publish, but we are not free to libel others.

- We are free to own firearms, but we are not free to carry a loaded gun into a classroom and point it at children.

- We are free to assemble with others, but we are not free to plot the overthrow of our government.

- We are free to drink liquor, but we are not free to do it when we are ten years old or to get intoxicated in public. The government even can tell a person where he or she can buy liquor, how much, and when.

A person is free to be "sexually liberated" and think slimy thoughts. A person is free to believe women and children are worthless objects to be used for another's pleasure. A person is free to let his or her mind be used as a toxic waste dump. But when a person carries out those thoughts, his freedom ends.

The argument I have heard most often as it relates to sexually explicit materials is, "Where is the harm?" Perhaps it is better to ask, "Where is the good?" If we continue down the path of pornography, will we enhance the attitude of children toward their sexuality? Will we better prepare a teenage boy for fatherhood? Will we teach young women to nurture a family?

> *A person is free to let his or her mind be used as a toxic waste dump. But when a person carries out those thoughts, his freedom ends.*

If one child is victimized, if one woman is raped and forever traumatized, if one teenage girl is exploited and emotionally destroyed because of pornography—then maybe this legacy of lust is not worth the risk.

Jesus is often depicted as mild mannered. But Jesus got angry over how people were treated, and he became livid when he saw people being exploited. There was nothing mild-mannered when he said, "It would be better for him to be thrown into the sea with a millstone tied around the neck than for him to cause one of these little ones to sin" (Luke 17:2). How we raise our children today when it comes to respecting themselves and others may determine the survival of our society.

Questions for Reflection and Discussion

1. Do you agree or disagree with this statement: "You can't legislate morality"? Why?

2. What have university studies in the United States and Canada told us about whether pornography is addictive? What is a "pornoholic"?

3. How do pornography and illicit sexual relationships cheapen sex?

4. According to the author, where do a person's individual freedoms begin and end?

5. In your opinion, what can individual Christians and churches do to combat pornography and sexually explicit materials in our society?

PART II

A Legacy Learned

SEVEN

Parents Do Matter

The legacy we leave often is shaped by the legacy we have inherited. The first school in which we enroll, and the most important one in shaping our future, is called home. A casual view of modern television programs might lead us to believe that parents don't matter. I contend that nothing matters more.

When Benjamin West was a boy, his mother left him in charge of his younger sister, Sally. Benjamin found bottles of colored ink and painted Sally's portrait. When his mother arrived home, she discovered spilled ink and ruined paper. But before she had the opportunity to raise her voice and scold Benjamin, she saw the picture. Then she planted an encouraging kiss on his cheek. Benjamin West would later say, "My mother's kiss made me a painter."

Every child's life is like a book of blank pages waiting to be written on. Something is written each day. A parent who exposes a child to hours of television, video games, unsupervised time on the Internet, and an occasional trip to church is not likely to raise a child whose value system will mirror that of the parent. The child will probably reflect the value system of the entertainment industry.

While researching an earlier book on juvenile violence, *Kids Who Kill*, I became increasingly conscious of the fact that children need parents who are informed and involved and who are invasive in their children's lives. There is no single fact that will explain why a child as young as eleven years old will commit mass murder. But one thing seems certain. The likelihood of this taking place decreases drastically when children have a stable home, good role models, and parents who are clearly more afraid *for* their children than afraid *of* their children.

> *Children need parents who are informed and involved and who are invasive in their children's lives.*

Too many parents fear angering or alienating their children. They convince themselves that it is love that lets their children refuse to answer questions about how their time is spent and who their friends are. They fool themselves into thinking they are being good parents when they don't hold their children accountable for their schoolwork and other activities.

The requirement of parents summed up in Ephesians 6:4 is simple yet profound: "Do not exasperate your children; instead, bring them up in the training and instruction of the Lord." Children should not be driven to exasperation by parents who make demands that are so impossible to achieve that the children are prevented from succeeding. There is a vast difference between breaking a child's rebellious will and breaking his or her spirit.

The goal of the parent should be to channel the energy of the child rather than destroy the creative and curious nature given by God that motivates the child to discover his or her purpose. We are further admonished to bring up our children in the training and instruction of the Lord. By both example and exhortation, parents are to nourish their children. Most values are caught and then taught. Our children are more likely to imitate what they see us do than what they hear us say.

The goal of the parent should be to channel the energy of the child rather than destroy the creative and curious nature given by God that motivates the child to discover his or her purpose.

I will always remember one incident that occurred during my years as a pastor when my children were young. One day upon hearing loud voices in the living room, I peered around the corner to observe my three children, ranging at the time in age from three to nine, "playing church." They acted out a church service, including the singing, the preaching, and the important "taking the offering."

I was amused, but I also was touched by the realization that whether I liked it or not, my children were growing up to imitate me. Years later I would be gratified when each of my three children indicated an interest in politics and government.

The ultimate job of a parent is to train his or her replacement. If we left a million shares of a valuable stock but did not leave instructions on how to parent the next generation, how could we claim success? Our children do not need to be forced into proper behavior by being bullied to the point that they act out of terror rather than a desire to please.

A prison once gave each of the inmates a Mother's Day card so they would have the opportunity to offer a loving greeting to their mothers. Within a short time, every card was taken. The effort was such a success that the warden decided he would also provide Father's Day cards. But as Father's Day neared, not one card was taken. This is revealing if you're searching for the causes of an ever-expanding prison population. This country is plagued by disappearing dads.

When a father views his role as little more than a baby maker, it is doubtful he will take the time or expend the effort to nurture a child into a healthy, balanced adult. One of my most painful memories in counseling young children is hearing children as young as five years old blaming themselves for their parents' divorce. Too many children become convinced that their parents' inability to get along was because of them.

During the past two generations, children have gone from being an important economic asset to an economic liability. This has happened as we have moved from an economy based largely on agriculture to an economy based on industry and technology. In an agricultural society, children were farmhands. Each child had a role to play in the success of the family enterprise.

> *Children should grow up with various tasks to perform that contribute to the success of the family.*

Today's children have little responsibility for the success of the household. Too many of them hear how much they are costing rather than how much they are worth. Children should grow up with various tasks to perform that contribute to the success of the family. This gives a sense of worth to each member of the family. It also gives parents the opportunity to praise their children as they reach their goals.

Children imitate even when they do not understand what they are copying or the consequences of their actions. This was revealed to me when my daughter, Sarah, was about two years old. I have always been an avid reader. One evening while seated in a recliner with my daughter on my lap, I

One of the most important lessons we can teach our children is to be patient when waiting for the things that are really important.

was reading a book. She had one of her small picture books. To help turn the pages in my book, I would lick a finger in order to get a good grip on the page being turned.

After a few minutes, I looked at my daughter, who had decided to "read" her book. As her right hand reached out to turn the page, she carefully licked a finger on her left hand. She wasn't sure why she was doing this. It never occurred to her to use the moistened finger on the page. But somehow, licking a finger was important to her dad when he was reading, and therefore it was important to her.

One of the most difficult challenges is knowing when children are ready to be entrusted with higher levels of responsibility. A small child came home from his first day of school. His father was eager to hear about that first day of kindergarten until the child stunned him with the question, "Dad, what is sex?"

The father thought to himself, "I realize kids are being exposed to sex at a much earlier age, but I really wasn't expecting to have to explain the origin of life quite so soon." Then he took a deep breath and said, "Son, sit down. I will do my best to explain." He began to describe in detail the facts of life. He felt he had done a respectable job in explaining what sex was. When he finished, he asked his son, "Did that help? Do you now know what sex is?"

The boy replied it was interesting and then added, "On a form we got at school today, it asked what sex I am. I just needed to know if I'm an M or an F."

One of the most important lessons we can teach our children is to be patient when waiting for the things that are really important. Perhaps nothing is more challenging for a contemporary parent to explain than the lesson that things of great value sometimes take a great amount of time.

When I was eleven years old, I received my first guitar for Christmas. My parents had saved money for months to buy an electric guitar from the J. C. Penney catalog. The guitar and small amplifier cost a whopping $99 dollars in 1966. It was one of the happiest and most memorable experiences of my life. Like every other kid my age, I was convinced I could rival the Beatles and perhaps be the leader of a rock band, traveling the world and entertaining the masses. I soon discovered, however, that learning to play that guitar took work.

> *Things of great value take time. Patience is a virtue as well as a pathway to victory.*

Today that mail-order guitar sits in the Old State House in downtown Little Rock as part of a collection of memorabilia from governors. For many who come and see it, it probably represents little more than a kid's dream to be a musician. For me, though, it is a reminder that long before I ever played before an audience and heard the applause, I spent hours and hours in my room hearing only the complaints of a family whose members had to endure the throbbing sounds.

We live in a world where a meal can be microwaved in seconds and an Internet message can be transmitted halfway around the world almost instantly. But part of the legacy we must leave is raising children who understand that some things can't be rushed. Things of great value take time. Patience is a virtue as well as a pathway to victory.

Questions for Reflection and Discussion

1. Why is it important that children grow up with various tasks to perform that contribute to the success of the family?

2. In your opinion, why do children need parents? What purpose do parents serve and what role do they play in the lives of their children?

3. What does the author mean by this statement in referring to parents and children: "Most values are caught and then taught"?

4. What evidence do we see of the truth of this statement by the author: "This country is plagued by disappearing dads"?

5. What legacy did your parents leave you? Describe the legacy that you would like to pass along to your children.

EIGHT

The Faith Factor

"I tried faith; it just didn't work for me."

It's an excuse I've heard hundreds of times in hundreds of ways. It's sometimes expressed like this: "I've tried to forgive, but I just can't. I've given my best effort to love him, but it just isn't happening."

Our culture has taught us to be in a hurry. We order our food from a car window and eat it from a paper sack as we hurry to our next appointment, driving as fast as the traffic will allow. We demand that our computers run at the speed of light and take it personally if our airline flights are more than five minutes late. We barely remember the days when popcorn was popped by holding a pan over a hot stove and shaking it vigorously. We prefer a three-minute zap in the microwave.

One of the most compelling verses in the New Testament is James 1:3: "The testing of your faith develops perseverance."

Deep distortions have been made when it comes to the meaning of those simple words. But they mean just what they say. In order for faith to work, we have to test it. We probably will not do too well when we test it the first time and therefore will be forced to test it again and again.

During my teenage years and early adulthood, I longed for a faith that would catapult me above the pressures and problems of daily life. I believed real faith would either remove the problems from me or remove me from the problems. It seemed logical that if I pledged my love to God, I would be able to escape flat tires, sick kids, surly store clerks, bad-hair days, and severe indigestion after a large plate of enchiladas.

> *In order for faith to work, we have to test it.*

Somehow it never worked. I now realize the sun shines on the just and unjust alike, and it also rains on the good as well as the bad.

If we are a member of the human family, we will face extraordinary trials and testing. What we may not understand is that such tests are necessary, not because God needs to figure us out (he already knows what we are made of and how we will respond) but so we might have it revealed to us what we are about.

The only way a boat can be tested is to be placed in the water. The only way a rope can be tested is to be pulled. A bird does not test its wings by submitting to an analysis by an engineer but by leaving the nest and attempting to fly.

In the Epistle of James we're also told we can "consider it pure joy" (James 1:2) when we face such trials. If it isn't bad enough that we must face these trials in life, it gets worse when we're told to "consider it pure joy." We're not being encouraged to enter into a type of emotional denial. On the contrary, we're admonished to consider the joy of the ultimate outcome. The trial is not an end in itself but a pathway to deeper character.

A man passing by a friend asked, "How are you?"

His friend replied, "Not too bad under the circumstances."

The man asked, "Well, what are you doing under there?"

Indeed, we weren't designed to live "under the circumstances" but

> *We weren't designed to live "under the circumstances" but to get through the circumstances by living above and beyond them. The purpose of any test is not to make us fall but to make us fly.*

to get through the circumstances by living above and beyond them. The purpose of any test is not to make us fall but to make us fly. The results of our tests are never a surprise to God, but they're often a surprise to us. Many people have said after watching a close friend go through the trauma of cancer, "I feel so sorry for her. I just don't know how she does it. I could never maintain my faith in the midst of such tragedy."

None of us believe we can endure crises and problems until after we've actually endured them. The test wasn't particularly revealing to the Creator, who knows us so well that the hairs on our head are numbered. The purpose of the trial is to help me know just how much faith I have—to understand just how much tugging I can take before the tether breaks.

The Epistle of James exhorts us to "try" our faith. It means just that. We try loving, we try forgiving, we try believing—and we will probably not be very good at it the first several hundred times we try.

> *Knowledge is knowing what to do, but wisdom is knowing why and what next. God invites us to ask questions so we might develop wisdom and understanding.*

Several years ago, I was invited to speak to a group of young adults at a ski resort in New Mexico. Many of my friends had told me what a wonderful experience skiing would be, and I was looking forward to it. After falling off the lift, having to climb uphill, and spending most of the day tumbling through the snow, I concluded I was not called to be a professional skier. In fact, I promised God if I lived though this day I would never try skiing again.

That was more than twenty years ago, and I'm proud to say I've kept my promise. Since that time, I've had numerous invitations to go skiing. I try to make it very clear that I tried skiing and it's just not for me.

My daughter is the youngest of our three children, and she is now in college. It seems like only yesterday that she was learning to walk. Since she was the youngest, she could look around and see every family member walking. From her position crawling on the floor, she could easily observe how legs moved. I remember the day when after months of observation, she concluded it was time to take her first step.

She pulled herself up by the edge of a sofa and carefully pushed off to begin her first steps. There was glee in her eyes as she took her first step and part of another before crashing with her nose buried in the carpet.

She crawled to a corner of the room and with her arms folded looked up at me and said in a clear voice: "Dad, I tried walking, and it just doesn't work for me. I realize you, Mom, John Mark, and David can all walk, but as you can see I tried and I can't do it. I've studied it for months. I've given it my best effort. I wanted to, but you saw the results. I tried and failed. I can't walk. You'll have to carry me for the rest of my life."

Do you really believe that happened? Of course it didn't. The truth is that she tried again and again. Again she failed. Again she tried. This continued until she was so exhausted she literally went to sleep on the floor. The next day, she began the process again. Little by little, her one step became two and then three. It wasn't long before she was able to wobble all the way across the room. Then she was running, jumping, and going faster than either her mother or me.

I remember my own childhood and the painful memories of learning to ride a bicycle. Other kids in the neighborhood who were older already were riding bicycles. If they could do it, so could I. With great determination, I mounted the bicycle and fell. I fell numerous times trying to get the right balance. No matter how many times I scraped my elbows, I kept trying because I was determined to ride that bike.

Most of the things we do successfully in life come about because we're willing to try more than once. Whether it is walking, riding a bicycle, forgiving, loving, or believing, we rarely succeed on our first try. Many of us will experience far more failures than successes. We'll become what we practice being. If we practice being loving, caring, faithful, giving, and forgiving, we'll become like that. If we practice selfishness, impatience, rudeness, greed, anger, and lust, we can rest assured that we'll become that as well.

The Bible urges us to "try our faith," but it also reminds us that when we try our faith we become overcomers and conquerors. We're encouraged to ask questions so we may understand what we're experiencing and why. Some of the best news in the Bible is that God urges us to ask questions: "If any of you lacks wisdom, he should ask God, who gives generously to all without finding fault, and it will be given to him" (James 1:5).

Knowledge is knowing what to do, but wisdom is knowing why and what next. God invites us to ask questions so we might develop wisdom and understanding. A big mistake in developing a sense of perseverance is that sometimes we're content asking God for information rather than asking him for wisdom.

When my oldest son John Mark was about three years old, he managed to get a big splinter in his foot. I looked at the foot and told him I would remove the splinter. The next several minutes were some of the most unpleasant I've ever experienced as a parent. John Mark screamed, fought, pleaded, and resisted. I did my best to explain that removing the splinter would not be painful unless he

> *A person does not become a confident believer in one sudden Damascus-Road experience. He or she becomes a person of faith and perseverance by trying and then trying again and again.*

moved his foot abruptly, causing me to stab the tweezers into his heel.

Although John Mark had the information he needed, he lacked confidence in my ability to remove the splinter. I thought we would either have to amputate his foot or have him put under a general anesthetic to bring this nightmare to a conclusion.

Sometimes we have information about God, but if we lack confidence in that information we will struggle, resist, and do great damage to ourselves trying to get away from the experience. It is precisely for this reason that we're given the ability to ask God for wisdom. We're free to ask him questions and expect answers. We're told, "He will give his wisdom liberally." This means that God gives without thought of a return and that he will not belittle us for asking.

There is a caveat to this invitation. In fact, it is more of a condition. We're told if we ask, we must ask in faith and must not waver (James 1:6). Real faith is when we commit to following God's instructions before we even know what they are. We must have confidence in God rather than ourselves. This brings about a sense of peace and the capacity to be an overcomer. A person does not become a confident believer in one sudden Damascus-Road experience. He or she becomes a person of faith and perseverance by trying and then trying again and again.

You've heard the old adage, "practice makes perfect." That's true of virtually any discipline in life, whether playing the piano or forgiving people who have hurt us. We practice and then practice some more. Finally, what was once a struggle that required every ounce of concentration becomes so much a part of us that we do it with the effortless ease of a gold-medal figure skater.

Rest assured that no person starts the journey to championship with thousands of people cheering and a gold medal draped around his or her neck. There are thousands of painful falls on cold ice. The bystanders chuckle at the failures and never imagine that one day the last laugh will belong to the person on the ice.

Questions for Reflection and Discussion

1. What is the most recent personal experience you have been through in which your faith was put to the test?

2. What does it mean for a Christian to live "above the circumstances"?

3. What's the difference between asking God for information and asking him for wisdom?

4. In your opinion, what does it mean for a Christian believer to "try" his or her faith?

5. According to the author, we live in a society that expects instant results. How does this influence our thinking about faith?

NINE

Faith with a Future: The Religion of Right On!

History is to a culture what memory is to an individual. Without some sense of who we were, we're incapable of knowing who we are and who we will become. The fruit of our life is tied to the root of our life. Understanding something about our past helps us better understand the present and chart our future course.

Successful driving of a car involves paying attention to what you see through the windshield as well as what you see in the rearview mirror. While the windshield covers the front of the vehicle and allows you to see what is ahead, the rearview mirror is only a small piece of glass that gives you the ability to see what is behind.

There is a lesson here. While it is important to glance in the rearview mirror from time to time, it's more important to keep our eyes focused on the path ahead. A person who fails to glance at the past is in

> *While it is important to glance in the rearview mirror from time to time, it's more important to keep our eyes focused on the path ahead.*

danger of losing perspective and perhaps being overcome by the unexpected. But a person who looks constantly at the past and fails to pay attention to the road ahead is destined for collision and disaster.

Part of leaving a legacy is understanding where we were, where we are, and how important both of those are in determining where we're going. Savoring the successes of the past can be satisfying, but we must not camp out in the comfort of memories. Many aspiring college students flunk out because they believe success in high school leads to automatic success at the university level. The dedication and perseverance it took to turn the tassel at high school graduation is intensified in college.

I've observed many people who peaked in their late teens. They believed all the compliments showered upon them by well-meaning people who told them they could sing like Mariah Carey or throw a football like Joe Montana.

I've watched sadly as gifted young people froze their talents at age nineteen because they believed they were as good as their admirers claimed. Imagine how ridiculous it would be for me to assume that because I took an aspirin last week I don't have to worry about a headache today. Even more absurd is the notion that after forty-five years of breathing and having my heart keep me alive, I could give my lungs and heart the day off as a reward for their years of faithful, consistent labor. I would be dead within minutes after my heart stopped beating and my lungs quit functioning.

Successfully having done anything yesterday means absolutely nothing when it comes to successfully doing something today or tomorrow.

Many people hope past successes in business relationships and even their successes in spiritual devotion to God can be translated into success tomorrow. The moment I stop exercising those disciplines of life, I stop growing and start dying. Genuine faith does not allow me to consider the disciplines of life to be an event. They're an ongoing process. My past successes guarantee nothing when it comes to my future endeavors.

> *No person is a failure because he failed. A failure is a person who stops trying.*

By the same token, while some of us need to forget our past successes, others need to forget their past failures. No person is a failure because he failed. A failure is a person who stops trying. Many people are paralyzed not by their inability to perform but by their unwillingness to stop staring at the road behind them and start looking at the road ahead.

Are there failures in your past? Go ahead and take a look at them. Then put your eyes on the road ahead, shift to drive, and hit the accelerator.

Our past sins and mistakes can't be changed. Some will leave scars on us as well as others. But after we have made responsible efforts to right wrongs, made restitution, and asked the forgiveness of those we've hurt and offended, we need to leave dead things buried.

My family once had a parakeet named Cookie. I'm not sure how long Cookie had been in the family. It was as far back as I could remember. When I was about four years old, Cookie died. My sister and I decided Cookie deserved a proper burial. We took an old shoebox, turned it into a casket, and conducted an impressive funeral service. We carefully dug a grave in our backyard, placed the shoebox containing Cookie in the grave, and covered it with dirt to bring closure to our relationship with this family fixture.

After a few weeks, my four-year-old curiosity could not be contained. I wondered how Cookie was getting along in her earthly habitat. Without seeking counsel from my older sister, I took it upon myself to do some digging to see how Cookie was getting along. To this day, I remember my horror at seeing the condition of that bird several weeks after what I thought was a proper burial. As bad as Cookie's death had been, digging her up only made it worse.

Once we've confessed our sins, received forgiveness, and cleared the air as best we can, it's time to determine that we'll never go back and dig up what is dead. Digging up the sins and failures of the past will be unimaginably bad. We cannot allow our past experiences to intrude on our present experiences. If we do, our legacy will amount to little more than painful memories and lost opportunities.

Many people struggle with intense guilt over past failures. All people do things they regret. But guilt robs you of the energy you need to carry on the duties of today. In essence, guilt is using up today's resources on past actions. God never intended us to be overwhelmed with energy-draining guilt. This is why he made provisions for forgiveness and restoration.

> *God never intended us to be overwhelmed with energy-draining guilt. This is why he made provisions for forgiveness and restoration.*

Forgiveness and restoration do more than cleanse our past. They empower our present.

During my first year as a pastor in Pine Bluff, Arkansas, I received a book from a major publishing company. I had not ordered the book, and there was neither a bill nor an explanation for the shipment. I assumed it was a promotional gift from the publisher sent to pastors in hopes they would buy an additional twelve books in the series.

When we think we can't handle the guilt any longer, our best course is to quit trying to confront it ourselves and to take it directly to the top.

The following month, the second book in the series arrived. Again, there was neither a bill nor an explanation. The third month, the third book arrived. This time there was a bill for all three of the books. Since I had not ordered the series, I was confident it was a mistake. I wrote the publishing house, informing them I would be happy to return the books if they would send me a shipping label and instructions for proper return.

My next contact with the company was when the fourth book in the series arrived. Thinking my letter had not gotten there in time to stop the fourth book, I waited. The fifth month saw another book arrive.

I wrote the publisher again and asked for a shipping label so I could return all five books. The next month, I received a sixth book and a bill for all books in the series thus far. I sent a third letter. You guessed it. In the seventh month, I got the seventh book and a bill for all seven books. This time, the billing letter was more aggressive. I was now receiving past-due notices for books I had never ordered and had tried to return.

I mailed yet another letter, but the eighth and ninth months resulted in the eighth and ninth books in the thirteen-month series being sent. I tried several long-distance telephone calls. Each time, I was assured the situation would be corrected. By the time the twelfth book had arrived, my account had been turned over to a collection agency, which threatened harsh action if I didn't pay the publisher immediately for books I had never ordered and seemed unable to return.

> *Faith ensures that the power of the living God through Jesus Christ works from the inside to equalize the outside pressure.*

I made one final try. A little research yielded the name of the president of the publishing company. I wrote him a letter in which I outlined the one-year saga and my futile attempts to get someone's attention at his company. I added that my church spent thousands of dollars each year purchasing literature. If this was how the company operated, I told him, I would do my best to ensure my church and any other churches I could contact avoided doing business with the company.

Less than a week later, my secretary informed me the gentlemen to whom I had written the letter was on the phone. Considering my past dealings with the company, I wasn't sure if he was calling to correct the situation or to announce that he was sending two goons over to rearrange my face.

Much to my relief, he apologized profusely and indicated that his own research had found the many errors on their part. After he acknowledged I had ordered nothing and therefore owed nothing, he told me he wanted me to keep the entire series of thirteen books. In addition, he would also send a commentary set I had long wanted but couldn't afford. He said if I had problems with his company again to simply use his name and ask that any questions be directed to him.

Two days later, a twenty-volume commentary arrived. It remains one of my most frequently used resource materials. The company president was true to his word. I was never billed again for the thirteen-book series and was never billed for the commentary set.

In a sense, guilt is being billed for sins we either didn't commit, have already paid for, or don't have the resources to pay for. Guilt drains us of faith, energy, and hope. When we think we can't handle the guilt any longer, our best course is to quit trying to confront it ourselves and to take it directly to the top.

When we take our problems to God, not only is he willing to take care of them, but he does something absolutely wonderful for us. He tells us if we're ever overburdened with guilt again that we should not attempt to deal with it by ourselves. We're to refer everything to him and allow him to deal with it. Ridding us of strength-robbing guilt is one of God's greatest gifts.

Questions for Reflection and Discussion

1. How does understanding our past help us better understand the present and chart our future course?

2. What happens to people when they stop learning and forging ahead and live off their accomplishments from the past?

3. What does the author mean by this statement? "Genuine faith does not allow me to consider the disciplines of life to be an event. They're an ongoing process."

4. Is there some past failure in your life that you need to put behind you? How does a person move beyond his or her failures and mistakes?

5. How does God's forgiveness and restoration cleanse our past and empower our present?

TEN

Faith without a Future: The Religion of Right Now

Real faith is not only getting beyond our past; it's recognizing that faith is an ongoing process. None of us "have arrived." At best, we can say we're "on the way." A big mistake many people make is the notion that at any given moment we're going to be complete and thus relieved from the prospect of additional construction. That is not and will never be the case.

Years ago I attended the Institute in Basic Life Principles led by Bill Gothard, who has become a dear, personal friend. His seminars have helped millions of people cope with the practical issues of living a life of faith. At the completion of the seminar, I was given a button on which this message appeared: B.P.W.M.G.I.N.F.W.M.Y. We were told to keep that message in mind. It stands for, "Be Patient with Me. God Is Not Finished with Me Yet."

What a wonderful reminder that while I'm not everything I want to be, I'm not all the things I once was. Our lives are filled with pressure and stress. This is not necessarily bad. Stress and tension, properly balanced, actually give us strength. A muscle never stretched and tested will become useless, but one that is stretched too far will tear and leave you writhing in pain.

The submarine is an amazing vessel. It would collapse like a paper cup under the extraordinary pressure placed on its hull if not for the internal pressure that equalizes the pressure from outside. Faith in our lives does not exempt us from external pressure. Faith ensures that the power of the living God through Jesus Christ works from the inside to equalize the outside pressure, giving us strength and keeping us from collapsing like a paper cup.

> *Real faith takes care of what was and empowers us for what is. It also assures us of what will be.*

Real faith involves having something in the distance to motivate us and keep us moving, as the apostle Paul admonished in his Epistle to the Philippians. We should "press on toward the goal" (Phil. 3:14). Imagine the Olympic swimmer as he propels his body forward, stretching his chest, giving every ounce of energy to reach the goal.

There is nothing unholy about wanting to be a winner. The opposite is true: There is a great deal unholy about not wanting to be a winner. One of the most inspiring films I've seen is the true story of Eric Liddell, an Olympic champion. Eric was a devout believer, but he never thought of his faith as something that would cause him to hold back and allow others to run ahead of him. He viewed his talents as an empowering gift that allowed him to run and win not for his own glory but for God's glory.

Faith gives us a focus for our future, helps us move in the direction of our destiny, and gives us the capacity to continue working toward a worthy legacy.

A man who had experienced constant failures in life had a habit of saying again and again, "If only." After hearing this endlessly, a friend said, "Stop saying that. Instead say, 'Next time.'" Real faith takes care of what was and empowers us for what is. It also assures us of what will be.

Question for Reflection and Discussion

1. Do you agree with this statement by the author: "Stress and tension when properly balanced actually give us strength"? Why or why not?

ELEVEN

Winning an Election, Losing a Generation

Politics has always been a contact sport. It has increasingly become a demolition derby, with each contestant entering the arena and then engaging in a series of crashes. Whoever remains standing is declared the winner. The best person with the superior ideas is often less important than the most creative advertising campaign and the largest war chest. Add in the cynicism of the media and the fact that so many political opponents are willing to play hardball. All of this means that running for public office is certainly not for the faint of heart.

I may not always like the process of politics, but the end product is public policies that lay the track upon which the next generation will move forward. No matter how idealistic a person is when entering the political arena, I can attest from personal experience there's always a temptation to make decisions that will affect the next election rather than chart the best course for the next generation. It's easy to justify such an attitude by telling yourself that if you don't get reelected, you won't be able to have an impact on future policy development. Our society increasingly demands measurable results in a short time. Being in public office is now about building a resume of accomplishments rather than laying the foundation for a lasting legacy that will result in a lifetime of change.

I try to visit public schools, preferably elementary schools, as often as possible. One of my primary reasons for visiting schools is not so much to introduce the students to a governor as it is to help remind me of what's really important about being in public office. My batteries are recharged when I'm around children. They are still filled with awe and wonder. They have not become like so many adults—angry, distrustful of others, filled with doubt and broken dreams.

Not long after becoming governor in 1996, I sat in a meeting room at a Little Rock hospital with almost fifty representatives of organizations that received Medicaid funds. We had asked them to assist us in finding areas in which we could save money in the Medicaid system. The state was rapidly approaching the point at which the needs would exceed the funding levels.

I listened for more than an hour as participants talked about the virtues of their organizations and why they needed to be given even more money. In a meeting designed to ask the participants how they could live with less, each found a way to articulate how they couldn't live without more.

I called on a quiet lady across the room who lifted her hand to be recognized. What she said in the next few minutes stirred something in me that would change my views and the agenda for tens of thousands of Arkansas children. She was Amy Rossi, executive director of Arkansas Advocates for Children and Families. She was known by regulars at the state capitol as a well-meaning person who tried to influence legislation so it would have more of a positive effect on children, especially those from poor families.

I had heard from people who wanted more tax dollars for their organizations, but her plea was refreshingly different. She wasn't there to ask for more money for an organization. She was there to remind us of a serious need in our state. She spoke passionately about the 110,000 Arkansas children whose parents were working and had avoided welfare but whose income was not enough to afford adequate health insurance for their children.

These kids fell into an unfair trap. They were the children of parents who earned too much to qualify for Medicaid and not enough to afford quality private health insurance plans. These were children whose chronic illnesses often were going undiagnosed and untreated.

Amy's plea might have been filed away with the other good ideas I regularly hear, but I couldn't stop thinking about those children. I realized the only thing that separated them and me was forty years. Fortunately for me and my family, the cost of insurance and medical care was not nearly as high in the 1950s and 1960s as it is now. It occurred to me that many children perhaps were being penalized because their parents had worked their way above the poverty line.

Subsequent meetings with the director of the Arkansas Department of Human Services, Tom Dalton, and state Medicaid director Ray Hanley brought forth a simple but revolutionary idea that gave the children of working parents preventive care. The ARKids First program was born. I introduced it to the Arkansas legislature in January 1997. It passed without a negative vote in either the House or the Senate.

I remember coming up with the name of the program while seated at my desk at the state capitol, feeling a true sense of inspiration. When the legislation was approved, I had the pleasure of signing the bill while seated at a small table surrounded by children at a downtown Little Rock day care center. The children were drawing pictures with crayons.

As I prepared to sign the bill, I found myself reaching for one of the crayons and probably made history by being the first person to sign a bill into law with a crayon rather than a pen. The spontaneity of the moment took hold, and the crayon became one of the symbols of the plan.

Since its conception in 1997, the ARKids First program has been incredibly successful in insuring more than sixty thousand children whose families probably could not have otherwise afforded preventive health care. By the time Congress passed its own children's health initiative months later, our program was up and running. Many of our citizens actually welcomed the small copayment that was required since it gave them a sense of shared responsibility and a feeling of not being "on welfare."

It's less expensive to prevent a problem than it is to try to fix it once it has grown into something much larger.

The real value of ARKids First will not be seen immediately, but I'm convinced it's less expensive to prevent a problem than it is to try to fix it once it has grown into something much larger. The value of ARKids First will be easier to see over the decades as children grow up not having missed school because of chronic illnesses. Is it costly? It's not as costly as having large numbers of sick children.

Another initiative we've promoted heavily in Arkansas is the Smart Start program, which puts a major emphasis on high standards and accountability while focusing on reading, math, and character-based education in the early grades. With Arkansas consistently ranked near the bottom in educational achievement, creating and implementing a statewide initiative that refocuses public education is an important task.

Like the ARKids First program, the real value of Smart Start will not be evident by the next election. It will take more than a year or two to see what happens when children grow up in a public education system where there are no excuses for failure, where the standards are raised instead of lowered, where individual students and schools are held accountable.

> *The politics of "right now" too often have robbed our citizens of the changes needed to make their lives better.*

There is a temptation among public officials to implement programs with an eye toward short-term results. This is an age of "micropolicies," the launching of which provide colorful backdrops for television cameras. Most of these programs do little in the long run to improve our country.

The longer I serve as governor, the more I try to remind myself that my most important decisions are not those that will affect the next election. They're those that will affect the next generation. If public officials had fought for generational programs fifty years ago, my state might not be one of the poorest in the country. The politics of "right now" too often has robbed our citizens of the changes needed to make their lives better.

Our Arkansas prison system is one of the most efficient in the country in terms of cost. We spend an average of about $14,000 per year on each inmate, far below the national average. But consider that for the same amount of money we spend to keep someone in a prison, we could enroll a student in any college or university in the state, pay full tuition, pay room and board, buy books, and still provide some spending money. Few things grieve me more than having to build more prisons to meet the demand that drugs and crime have placed on the Arkansas Department of Correction.

I can't help but wonder how many people who languish in our prisons today might have been learning in our colleges and universities if we had placed a higher priority on building a fence at the top of the hill to keep them from falling off. This would have been preferable to spending big money on ambulances at the bottom of the hill to pick up what was left after they fell.

In a culture that's addicted to pleasure and immediate gratification, it's increasingly difficult to live in a way that will impact lives long after we're gone.

I'm determined to fight the demons of instant gratification so I can dedicate my tenure in office to adopting policies that might not have an immediate result but will help the people of my state beyond my lifetime.

Not everyone governs a state. But everyone makes decisions that affect others. Just as politicians are tempted to live only for the next election, many Americans live for the next vacation or even the next weekend. In a culture that's addicted to pleasure and immediate gratification, it's increasingly difficult to live in a way that will impact lives long after we're gone.

Imagine the difference in government alone if we made decisions based on how they impacted the next generation rather than influenced the next election.

A young man rapidly approached his birthday and could sense something significant was going on. A week before his birthday party, he found the garage door locked. On his birthday, he was escorted to the kitchen, where he was met by his parents, grandparents, and a number of aunts and uncles. The family then gathered near the garage door and watched as the boy's father placed the key in the padlock and opened the door.

A large section of a tree—more than five feet tall and at least a foot thick—greeted the boy and his family. As he approached the tree, he noticed it had been meticulously polished. He also noticed small signs that noted the dates at which rings of the tree had formed and the connection to events in history. One ring was labeled "The Emancipation Proclamation, 1863." Another marker showed the year when his mother and father had married.

As the boy studied the rings, he learned about the history of his family and also gained clues about the history of his race. The boy had been given something far more valuable than a piece of a tree. This gift taught him about his past.

The boy's name was Alex Haley, who grew up to write the best-selling novel *Roots*. This book was adapted into the most significant television miniseries in our country's history.

As we work, raise our children, and make daily decisions, we need to ask if they are for the immediate or for the ultimate good. Imagine the difference in government alone if we made decisions based on how they impacted the next generation rather than influenced the next election.

Questions for Reflection and Discussion

1. Do you agree that public officials should strive for long-term solutions to problems rather than immediate and short-term results? Why or why not?

2. Why does the author declare that "running for public office is certainly not for the faint of heart"?

3. Why is it tempting to public officials to make short-term policy decisions rather than decisions that affect the next generation?

4. When it comes to matters of public policy, why is it less expensive to prevent a problem than it is to try to fix it once it has grown into something much larger?

5. Have you ever made a decision that worked for the short term but turned out to be a bad decision several years down the road? What can we do to keep from making such short-sighted decisions?

TWELVE

The Ditto Factor

The trail we leave behind in life is largely determined by the manner in which we lead in life. One doesn't have to be governor to be in a position of leadership. Being a leader is not necessarily the same as being the chief executive officer of a major corporation, the president of a large club, or the chairman of a committee. Anyone who is a parent is a leader of perhaps the most important corporation of all—the family.

I've been able to attend many leadership courses through the years. I've also been able to participate in a number of community leadership organizations. But rarely have I been confronted with anything that could not have been gleaned from a thorough reading of the Book of Proverbs and the Sermon on the Mount. Let's examine some requirements for leaders.

> *To flee youthful lust means to run like a sprinter from any impulse that is characteristic of immaturity.*

Requirements of Leadership

Before we get in front of some things as leaders, we need to get away from others. The apostle Paul urged Timothy to "flee the evil desires of youth" (2 Tim. 2:22). This verse is often used to hammer away at teenagers about the need to avoid premarital sex. But the command is actually much larger in scope. To flee youthful lust means to run like a sprinter from any impulse that is characteristic of immaturity. It can refer to any desire common among those who are immature.

Such traits include impatience, a quickness to argue, unrealistic ambitions, willingness to lose a war in order to win a battle, and rejection of tradition and experience. It can mean simply the know-it-all attitude.

While driving on the freeway one day, I spotted a bumper sticker that made me laugh out loud. It said, "Hire a teenager while he still knows everything."

It's irritating but totally predictable when a child asks on a long trip, "Are we there yet?" We also expect children to argue about who sits near the window. And we're not surprised when small children argue the virtues of eating ice cream instead of vegetables as a main course. They might even contend that a daily bath is unnecessary, though we can smell them before we see them.

While all of this might be predictable for a child, it is still important to flee youthful lust as a person grows. Jimmy Taylor refused to get out of bed one morning and proclaimed, "I'm not going to school today. I hate school, and I'm not going back. The kids hate me, the teachers hate me, I hate the food, and I'm tired of being called names. Just give me one good reason I should go." Mrs. Taylor replied, "You're going to school today whether you want to or not because you're forty-six years old and you're the principal."

A mark of maturity is when we perform even the unpleasant, mundane tasks with regularity and without complaint.

A mark of maturity is when we perform even the unpleasant, mundane tasks with regularity and without complaint. A person who has to force himself out of bed to go to work each day is not likely to leave a legacy. The person who has to be begged to perform basic responsibilities is acting like a child. When it comes to leadership, it is important that we run *from* some things before we run *to* some things.

Another paradox of leadership is that before leaders lead, they must learn to follow. Some wag said that "the self-made man is the world's greatest example of unskilled labor." Following our instincts while ignoring our Creator is a foolish course.

One of the greatest mysteries of adolescence is how a fifteen-year-old can be pressed into the habits of smoking, drinking, reckless driving, and promiscuous activity through the urging of another teenager. The rational thing would be to follow those who have a successful track record. Would you be willing to put your life in the hands of a surgeon, knowing the surgeon had never performed the procedure you needed?

When speaking to student groups, I often ask, "How many of you would like to go with me?" The natural response is strange looks before someone finally asks, "Where are you going?" I have few takers when I respond, "You'll just have to trust me." My point is to remind them that if they don't know where they're being led, it might be best not to follow.

One of the reasons it is rational to follow the Creator is that wherever he leads us, we can be assured he has been there before. He knows the path.

Just as leaders need to flee certain activities, they also need to forsake arguments. While it is appropriate to ask questions and gain insight, we're never in a position to lead if our opportunities to move forward are hindered by an argumentative spirit.

All of us know people who believe that every issue needs opposition. There is a difference between asking questions and questioning everything. The

person who argues about every decision and every opinion not only loses
companionship but also loses the
capacity to be a companion during a
crisis. It's hard to visit a hospital room
and offer comfort to a person with
whom you've been at odds on virtually
every issue.

When we express an opinion, we
must do so in the right spirit. Having a
short temper and always being ready to
fight is more than unbecoming of a
leader. It ultimately is the undoing of a
leader.

We're told in the Scriptures to exer-
cise meekness, gentleness, and humility
(Col. 3:12). But there is a difference
between being meek and being weak.
Meekness means "teachable." In any leader's life,
there must be a proper balance between being fed
knowledge and feeding knowledge and wisdom to
others. We should lead by loving, not shoving.

The real job of leaders is to make others successful rather than using others to make themselves successful. The art of bringing out the best in others will
multiply your own capacity for success. Look around
and notice that the most successful people you know
tend to be those who have invested their lives in others. By helping those around them rise, leaders also
succeed.

> *The real job of leaders is to make others successful rather than using others to make themselves successful.*

One of the great truths of leadership is that true leaders never ask of others what they're unwilling to do themselves. The attitude of "feeding while we're leading" recognizes that a humble, teachable heart is a prerequisite to gaining the confidence of others.

> *It's not enough for us to be right when we speak the truth. We must also speak the truth in the right spirit.*

Many people want to hear from God and be assured their life's plan is being carried out properly. One way to ensure we're acting under God's direction and not under our own power is by following the real lessons of leadership. When we do that, we're more likely to have knowledge of the specific steps God wants us to take. It should be our goal to make God's plan known in word as well as spirit.

In the 1970s I worked for James Robison, head of a global mission organization. While traveling to a speaking engagement, James handed me an article and asked me to pass it to his teenage daughter, Rhonda. Clowning around, I thrust the folder containing the article in front of Rhonda and said, "Here! Your dad said for you to read this."

James heard me and said, "Mike, I did ask you to give it to her, but I didn't tell you with that tone or spirit. It's not enough that you communicate what I said. It's equally important that you communicate it in the spirit in which I said it."

110

I learned a vital lesson that day. It's not enough for us to be right when we speak the truth. We must also speak the truth in the right spirit if we're genuinely interested in having God's word revealed to us or if we're interested in correctly revealing it to others. We must say it in the manner the Father said it lest we communicate the wrong message in the wrong spirit, bringing the wrong result.

> *Leading others out of the darkness and into the light gives us the capacity to leave behind something greater than money or property. We leave behind better people.*

Repentance may be an old-fashioned word, but it would do us all good to recognize the significance of turning from the things in our lives that hurt and hinder us. Real leadership will cause those around us to turn from what is wrong and toward what is right. Unfortunately, some people are more interested in winning arguments than winning converts to the correct course of action. But the Bible doesn't say, "He who wins arguments is wise." It says, "He who wins *souls* is wise" (Prov. 11:30).

The effectiveness of our leadership will be determined by the number of people who come to a knowledge of God because of us and who do what's right. Our effectiveness also will be determined by the number of people who reject God because of us and who do what's wrong. Good leadership will cause others to follow us down the proper path rather than down the road to rebellion.

As leaders, we will make some mistakes, and some of these will be quite harmful. True leadership will give us the capacity to help people recover from the traps into which they fall. It's not a disgrace when people stumble into a trap, but it's unacceptable when they seem content to stay there.

We weren't designed by God to be taken captive by bad habits, attitudes, and behaviors that lead to our destruction. Leading others out of the darkness and into the light gives us the capacity to leave behind something greater than money or property. We leave behind better people.

Questions for Reflection and Discussion

1. Do you believe the family is the most important institution of all? Why?

2. Think of a person who has been a helpful influence in your life—your mother, father, or some other person. Did she invest her life in herself or in you?

3. In whose life are you investing yourself?

PART III

A Legacy Lived

THIRTEEN

The Power of Being Positive

On the way to work in 1988, I heard a catchy song on the radio. For the next several weeks, I heard it repeatedly. As it turned out, it was a big hit, sold more than ten million copies, and was nominated for a Grammy award. It was an odd song that admonished us over and over to "don't worry, be happy!" Written and performed by Bobby McFerrin, the song had such an impact that the February 27, 1989, issue of *Newsweek* carried a two-page spread about its popularity. Even Bloomingdales opened a "don't worry, be happy" shop.

Being a positive person has been the focus of countless books, seminars, sermons, video series, and personal counseling sessions. If we're going to leave a legacy, most of us would prefer to leave something that future generations would want to pick up and carry on. There is power in being positive, not only for the immediate but also for the ultimate.

But one of the fallacies of the positive thinking movement is that being a positive person consists of working up enough emotion to ignore reality and talk yourself into believing that everything will be fine. It's true that a positive spirit will take the unpleasant experiences of life and make them more tolerable. But there is something even better as it relates to the ultimate outcome of life.

Our attitude does determine our altitude in many respects. If we believe we're going to succeed, we're much more likely to do so. If we're convinced we'll fail, we're rarely disappointed in our prediction. There are some principles we can apply to unleash the power of being positive.

Positive Principles

1. *Being positive originates in a peaceful mind.* Our thoughts really do control us. A Hindu trader once asked a missionary about the "shine" on his face: "What do you put on your face to make it shine?" When the missionary realized he was talking about his countenance, he explained the "shine" came from the inside, not the outside. Our hearts experience; our faces reflect. When we're at peace with our inner selves, this peace is projected in our expressions. People who look for good are usually able to find it. Those who see the worst in everything generally project anger and bitterness.

116

People tend to be most critical of the success of others in areas where they are weak. For example, I have observed that people who give the least are the most vocal in criticizing how money is spent. People who do the least work most often criticize the work being done. Those who have the fewest friends are those who are the least friendly. The power of being positive originates in a peaceful mind.

2. *The power of being positive is articulated through a pleasant mouth.* Our words reveal our hearts just as our countenance reflects our spirit. When Frederick Cappel was chief executive officer of AT&T, he grew weary of a talkative lady whose negative comments and questions dominated a discussion. In the fourth hour of a stockholders' meeting, the lady asked Cappel, "How much money did we give to charity?"

Cappel said, "About ten million dollars."

The lady replied, "I think I'm going to faint!"

Cappel responded to the delight of the audience, "Ma'am, that would be most helpful."

What fills our mind generally will flow from our mouths. When we've truly developed an attitude of being positive, it will be reflected in what we think as well as what we say.

3. *The power of being positive circulates by positive methods.* Acting with integrity is never out of style. Few of us respect a crook or a schemer. When it appears that a person of dubious character is succeeding, we're disappointed. We think it is a shame

> *The person who has a positive life will enjoy the successes of others. He will never delight in the failure of other people.*

that a person could achieve something good through bad deeds or behaviors. While virtually everyone takes pleasure in the success of an honest person, disappointment reigns at the triumph of a scoundrel. The person who has a positive life will enjoy the successes of others. He will never delight in the failure of other people. Negative people often hope to witness the failure of others.

4. *The power of being positive disintegrates personal misery.* Most of us have been around people who work harder to be unhappy and miserable than they would have to work to be successful. There is a story of a farmer who could always find the worst in every experience. One day while being complimented on a bountiful crop, he replied, "A bumper crop sure is hard on the soil." No one can share joy with a bitter-hearted person because there is no joy to share.

In the late 1980s, a book published by Villard Books captured the essence of such an attitude. It was titled *Negaholics*. The authors suggested that some people are addicted to negativism, generally because of their low self-esteem.

5. *Positive thinking is powerful medicine.* The *Journal of the American Medical Association* has

reported that pain sometimes can be treated successfully with "humor therapy." A Swedish study found significant relief, especially from muscle-bone disorders and from depression, when people added a healthy dose of humor. This should not be news to those who read the Bible. Proverbs 17:22 says, "A cheerful heart is good medicine, but a crushed spirit dries up the bones."

Medical science is finally beginning to affirm what the writer of Proverbs said several thousand years ago: Laughter is a great medicine. Dr. Redford Williams of Duke University has said that a Type A personality is not as prone to a heart attack as once thought. He advances the idea that it is not the personality as much as it is unresolved anger and hostility that puts stress on the human body.

The philosophy of life I've tried to adopt has proven to be especially helpful in a political career. It is this: "Take God seriously, but don't take yourself too seriously." It's easy to do just the opposite, placing a great deal of importance on what we do, what we think, where we go, and what people think of us while paying little

> *It is vitally important not only for our sense of legacy but also for our health that we take God seriously and lighten up about ourselves.*

attention to our relationship with the God from whom we came and to whom we will return.

It is vitally important not only for our sense of legacy but also for our health that we take God seriously and lighten up about ourselves. The world was here before we came, and it will continue to get along after we're gone.

During my freshman year at Ouachita Baptist University in the fall of 1973, the outbreak of the Yom Kippur War in the Middle East caused many theology students to surmise this was the beginning of the end and that the world soon would face its final chapter.

One of my fellow freshman scheduled an appointment with Dr. Vester Wobler, chairman of Ouachita's religion department, to announce he would be withdrawing from school because he could not justify sitting in a classroom while there were so many souls to save before the world ended. Dr. Wobler, one of the wisest men I've known, leaned back in his chair, pulled his glasses down on his nose, and said to my classmate: "My, my, I'm not sure how the good Lord has gotten along all these years without you."

A healthy sense of humor is an important ingredient for a person whose legacy will be attractive and desirable.

My father never made much money. He worked as a fireman to pay the rent and keep food on the table. He had to take a second job as a mechanic on his days off from the fire station. With him and my mother working, we had just enough money to get by but never enough to get ahead. When my father died in 1996, about all he had to leave my mother in a material sense was a house, a small life insurance benefit, a few personal items, and a shed filled with tools.

But he left something else that was priceless. He left us with a wonderful sense of humor. It was hard to appreciate how laughter filled our house until I grew older and realized not everyone's home is blessed with such humor. It's not that his Irish temper didn't come through occasionally. But no matter how little we had, we always had a home filled with laughter.

The Bible tells us we're created in God's image. If we have a sense of humor, it is because he does as well. I'm convinced he has a wonderful sense of humor as evidenced by some of the people he has created!

During my years as a pastor, I conducted more than four hundred funerals. I found the careful use of humor at a funeral service could be helpful in bringing peace to a family and easing the tension that such an occasion can bring.

One of the types of drugs most often prescribe today is antidepressant medication. In our state's Medicaid budget, it represents the fastest-growing drug cost. If we were to take the Bible at face value, we probably would discover that instead of reaching for medicine we would sometimes be better off reaching for a joke book. We might discover that humor really is healthy and adds to the power of being positive.

6. *The power of being positive culminates in a prosperous ministry.* I spend hours each month at receptions. I stand in a single place for long periods and meet people either in a formal receiving line or in a casual way for brief moments of conversation. During a campaign season, my wife Janet and I sometimes are involved in as many as three receptions in a single evening, standing for hours and meeting hundreds of people.

Most people find it hard to believe that I actually enjoy such experiences—with two exceptions. One is the pain it brings to my feet, knees, and back from standing for long periods. The other unpleasant aspect is when I encounter someone who uses the occasion for an extended complaint session.

> *There is power in a positive spirit. The person who has it and shares it is one who will leave a real legacy.*

We've all had the experience of being sandwiched between people who are determined to make everyone around them as miserable as they are. Most of us would rather have our hair set on fire than endure an endless stream of whining.

Positive people are welcome in almost every situation. By contrast, negative people make us want to flee. A person known for a quick wit, a kind word, a smiling face, and a willingness to listen is a valuable asset. I've known some people who thought there was very little they had to offer the world. They weren't outstanding singers, they didn't have the capacity to speak eloquently, they weren't tremendous administrators, and they didn't exhibit leadership skills. But they did have a positive zeal for life. Their presence did more to light up a room than a floodlight. There is power in a positive spirit. The person who has it and shares it is one who will leave a real legacy.

Questions for Reflection and Discussion

1. Have you ever known a person whom you considered a "negaholic"? Describe the characteristics of such a person.

2. According to the author, one characteristic of a leader is that he or she must be teachable. What is the most valuable recent lesson you have learned about life and leadership?

3. Why is it important for leaders to speak the truth as well as speak it in the right spirit?

4. Do you agree with this statement by the author: "A healthy sense of humor is an important ingredient for a person whose legacy will be attractive and desirable"? Why or why not?

5. Why is a know-it-all attitude a mark of immaturity? What are some additional characteristics of an immature person?

FOURTEEN

It's the Money, Honey

The dentist held the narrow silver instrument with a needle-like probe at the end. I was already nervous. When the sharp probe touched the tooth cavity, every muscle in my body stiffened. I let out an audible noise and sat straight up in the chair despite the significant levels of nitrous oxide I was inhaling though a rubber mask over my nose.

"Did that hurt?" asked the dentist. I wanted to reply, "Hurt? Why no, it felt great. In fact, I was hoping you could do that several more times. I just screamed and sat up in the chair to make sure you were having as much fun as I am."

As sensitive as that tooth was, people are even more sensitive about money. They're especially sensitive about anyone who tries to convince them to give any of it up. As a pastor and a political candidate, I've spent a great deal of my adult life finding creative, not-so-painful methods of getting people to feel good about parting with their money in order to finance a cause.

During the 1992 presidential campaign, a sign hung in the Bill Clinton campaign headquarters in downtown Little Rock. Placed there by a political consultant, James Carville, the sign proclaimed, "It's the economy, stupid." Political analysts believe the 1992 election was indeed more about people's attitudes toward the economy than any other issue.

Money not only drives elections; it also influences marriages, business relationships, and relations between nations. Our prisons in Arkansas are filled with people who killed others or tried to kill them because they wanted money that was not theirs.

Part of the legacy we'll leave depends on the manner in which we manage our money. Understanding the spiritual perspective on money is not difficult. We'll examine it by looking at man's requirement and God's response.

Man's Requirement

In the third chapter of Malachi, God's people were told they had abandoned God's law and their disobedience had brought a curse so severe that crops were failing and the economy was collapsing. The people of Malachi's day were unsure what sin they had committed.

In words that are as graphic as can be found anywhere in the Bible, the prophet told them they had robbed God (Mal. 3:8). In reality, it's impossible to rob God in a literal sense, but in the ancient Hebrew language the word means "to hide, defraud or supplant." Because the people of Malachi's day had kept what was supposed to be given to God in tithes and offerings, they were experiencing an unusual economic downturn. The real issue was not money but obedience.

The prophet understood correctly that 90 percent obedience is 100 percent disobedience. Setting aside 10 percent of earnings as a tithe was designed as a tangible expression of trust and confidence for the people. They needed to realize that having 90 percent of one's income with God's blessing is far superior to having 100 percent of one's income with his curse.

The prophet urged the people to "bring the whole tithe into the storehouse" (Mal. 3:10) and further challenged them to prove if God was in fact faithful. Can God be trusted to bail me out of poverty if I have not trusted him with my prosperity? The idea of managing money revolves around being a responsible steward of the resources you have. Stewardship is not a carefully packaged financial program of giving. It's a concept that recognizes we're not actually the owners of anything. We're mere managers of the things that are in our control.

> *Having 90 percent of one's income with God's blessing is far superior to having 100 percent of one's income with his curse.*

> *The person who recognizes his or her role as a steward understands that God owns and orders all things.*

Stewardship is the management of the time, talent, and treasure that God has given us. The person who recognizes his or her role as a steward understands that God owns and orders all things. He has a right to tell you what to do with the property that he has entrusted to your management.

Before the steward can manage "things," he must manage himself. God's requirement for us to give generously is not because he is needy but because we are needy. The legendary psychiatrist Dr. Karl Menninger said, "Generous people are rarely mentally ill."

God's Response

Giving and receiving are directly proportionate. It's as simple as the law of the harvest: We reap what we sow. Of course, not only is it true that we reap what we sow; we reap later than we sow. Further, we reap more than we sow. A person who claims to want to be more godlike is a person who should become as generous a giver as possible. When we give time, talent, and treasure, we most resemble the God whom we worship.

The one thing that's clear about the heavenly Father is that he has never been one to see how little he could get by with giving in order to meet the minimum requirements of being God. I've always worried about people who ask me what is the minimum they can give in order to meet what they believe to be God's demands.

Some people argue that the tithe is passé, that we do not live under Old Testament law. Frankly, tithing is not an expression of generosity. It's an expression of our minimum requirements. The Old Testament requirement was not abolished by New Testament grace. That's because grace always requires a greater devotion—not less devotion—than the law.

One of the remarkable surprises of the Bible is that we're told our giving should be "cheerful" (2 Cor. 9:7). I've often quipped there are many similarities between politics and church work. Large amounts of money must be raised for each. The primary difference is that in church

> *The one thing that's clear about the heavenly Father is that he has never been one to see how little he could get by with giving in order to meet the minimum requirements of being God.*

work you preach that God loves a cheerful giver. In politics you will accept money from a grouch!

Giving with a smile and enthusiasm most resembles the God who never regrets the gifts he gives us.

129

> *The manner in which we handle money doesn't reveal as much about our finances as it does the quality of our spiritual character.*

Giving like God is "source giving" rather than "sense giving." We give out of our understanding that God is the source of all we have rather than giving because it makes sense financially.

Malachi indicated giving would cause God to rebuke the "devourer" (Mal. 3:11). The manner in which we handle money doesn't reveal as much about our finances as it does the quality of our spiritual character. God can test our eternal trust by observing our temporal trust. It's difficult to believe we can trust God to deliver us from eternal death, but we're somehow unable to believe God can be trusted to get us out of debt.

Certainly God has not promised us personal wealth or what the world considers a high standard of living. But when we learn to give and give generously, we'll discover God is always capable of giving back more than we gave to start with.

True giving also involves a level of trust that comes when we don't seek to control every aspect of the gift. Malachi admonished the people to give to their spiritual "storehouse" (Mal. 3:10). People should give first and foremost to their local church, not only because of the practical needs of the church's ministry but because real giving means you don't control all uses of the money.

God wants to bless us and demonstrate to the world that he will provide for our needs. Some of the greatest stories of American wealth are about the generosity of individuals.

William Colgate, the founder of Colgate-Palmolive Corporation, was an extraordinarily generous man whose goal was more to give than to earn. As his business prospered, his giving not only increased in amount but also in proportion.

James Cash Penney, who launched the J. C. Penney retail empire, had given away millions of dollars before the Great Depression. When the collapse of the economy during the depression caused him to lose most of what he had built, a newspaper reporter asked him, "Mr. Penney, do you regret all those millions you gave away to charity now that you are virtually broke and have to start over?"

Penney replied, "My only regret was that I didn't give away more. The things I gave I still have in the way of hospitals, churches, and orphanages. It's the things I kept that were lost forever."

I've observed that some people resent the giving and receiving of personal wealth. But it also has been my careful observation that people tend to think of others as they think of themselves. The liar, for example, believes all people are liars and thus finds it difficult to accept the truth from anyone. The thief believes all others are stealing as well. It's only a matter of who will be caught and who will get away with it.

The person who is selfish believes all other people are selfish and thus is suspicious of those who have a generous, giving spirit, believing they must have an ulterior motive. Such a person cannot accept the fact that some people are generous because of the joy they receive from giving things away. But this principle makes perfect sense to a person with a generous heart. That person gives not in hopes of getting something in return but merely to be godlike.

> *In the true spirit of giving, the person who received a gift is not so much obligated to return the favor as he is to pass on a similar blessing to another.*

Public officials are confronted with rules on the giving and receiving of gifts. I think it's a good idea to disclose to the public the types and scope of gifts. Voters should be able to evaluate the relationships that those in public office have and decide whether the givers are exerting too much influence.

But the trend in many states is to regulate and even prohibit normal giving and receiving among friends and relatives. These rules often are made by those who don't understand that true giving is not about seeking to influence someone. In the true spirit of giving, the person who received a gift is not so much obligated to return the favor as he is to pass on a similar blessing to another. Thus, this transaction becomes an ever-expanding circle of compassion and generosity.

If money means a great deal to us, we will resent being asked to give it away. We'll resent everything we do give. And we'll resent it when other people give because this reveals our lack of a generous spirit. Since we're all going to leave this life as empty-handed as we were when we entered, learning to give things away develops God's generous spirit as part of our character. It also means practicing letting go of the things we'll ultimately let go of anyway.

The slogan of the 1992 presidential campaign—"It's the economy, stupid"—seems a little on the crude side. So maybe a "kinder and gentler" way to say it is this: "It's the money, honey."

Questions for Reflection and Discussion

1. How does the author define *stewardship?* Do you agree or disagree with his definition? Why?

2. In your opinion, what does it mean to be a "cheerful" giver?

3. Why are people so sensitive about money and the giving and receiving of money?

4. How is it possible for people to "rob" God, since he is the ultimate owner of the world and everything in it?

5. Does God's command of the tithe still apply to modern believers?

FIFTEEN

Using What You Have

The runaway success of the television game show *Who Wants To Be A Millionaire?* was a cultural phenomenon. Sociologists are trying to determine exactly what drives huge audiences to a simple game show in which contestants must answer increasingly difficult questions in an attempt to win one million dollars.

There's perhaps something in all of us that asks, "What would I do with one million dollars?" While most of us are quite confident of what we would do with the money, the bigger challenge in life is doing something responsible with what we do have.

Many of us believe our lives would be far more successful if we could change things that are beyond our power to change. If I were a foot taller, I might be able to play in the NBA. If I were more attractive, I might land a movie role. If I possessed great wealth, I would donate significant amounts to charity and make it possible for children to have lifesaving operations.

135

The God who placed us on this earth has a detailed inventory of our personal resources. It's much more appealing to fantasize about what we would do with unheld treasures than it is to be faithful to the riches we actually possess. Using what we have rather than what we wish for is especially important in three areas of life.

Use What's in Your Head

It's a natural temptation to assume that what we have will not make much difference in the world. We do, in fact, possess the power to leave our footprints in the world in a powerful way.

When Jesus fed five thousand people with a boy's lunch, he did so by taking what was available and believing that with God's strength it would be adequate (Mark 6:30–44). At first, the disciples who were with Jesus saw only a need and couldn't imagine any resource to meet it. This was true, although they had seen their Master speak to a storm and calm it and had seen him heal the critically ill.

The disciples had even seen Jesus take something as simple as water and turn it into the finest wine. They lived with a type of "spiritual amnesia." They were having a difficult time recalling the miracles they had witnessed and thus were limiting their options to what they knew within themselves.

136

It's a natural temptation to assume that what we have will not make much difference in the world. We do, in fact, possess the power to leave our footprints in the world in a powerful way. We perhaps have said, "I would never make it through the pain and agony of that kind of surgery," although we later did just that. Just when we wonder how we might handle the loss of a job and the income that goes with it, we end up actually losing our job and find out things about ourselves that we never knew.

Christian author and Holocaust survivor Corrie Ten Boom told about when she would take childhood train trips with her father. During a particularly anxious moment in Corrie's life, her father calmed her by asking, "When do I give you your ticket for the train ride?"

She replied, "Just before we board the train."

Her father said, "Well, that is how God works."

God doesn't give us grace for the experiences we don't face—only for the experiences we do face. He never fails to equip us for the experiences we have.

Adequacy for any task is not found solely in our capacity for the moment. We must know God will supply the energy we need to survive and succeed.

Use What's in Your Hand

When Jesus fed the multitudes, he did not ask the location of the nearest grocery store. He asked the disciples, "How many loaves do you have?" (Mark 6:38). As the disciples surveyed their inventory, all

> *It's faithfulness that makes us successful rather than the other way around — our successes don't make us faithful.*

they could come up with was the equivalent of five biscuits and a couple of small fish. By the biblical description, that's the lunch of a boy, hardly enough for an adult and woefully inadequate to feed thousands of people.

The disciples began to argue among themselves because they could focus only on what they had. And in their minds, that was inadequate. But Jesus took a boy's lunch and transformed it into enough food to feed the multitudes.

We are not called to be successful as much as we're called to be faithful. In the great scheme of things, it's faithfulness that makes us successful rather than the other way around—our successes don't make us faithful.

Leaving a legacy is not so much the result of great achievements as it is our faithfulness. In faith, we can give God our experiences, being reminded of our survival thus far, taking an inventory of our present resources, and believing God will enable us to be adequate as we carry out his directions.

Use What's in Your Heart

When Jesus took the small amount of food and thanked God for it, it was exactly the opposite of what most of us do when confronted with inadequate resources for the tasks we face. Jesus thanked God for what we would have complained about. We often find ourselves making a speech to God about the inadequacy of what we have rather than thanking him for stretching our possessions until the need is met.

The miracle performed by Jesus in feeding thousands of people revealed to the disciples that what appears to be insufficient is more than capable of meeting whatever needs exist. Not only did Jesus thank God for the little that was there, he also ordered that it be distributed. On the surface, it would appear that when a person has little, it's best to hold it. But it's giving that releases the power of a little to become a lot.

> *On the surface, it would appear that when a person has little, it's best to hold it. But it's giving that releases the power of a little to become a lot.*

It's easy to imagine the influence we might have if only we were blessed with greater strength, wealth, or health. The energy we use imagining what *could be* often robs us of what *should be*.

Several years ago it was my pleasure to know a man named Bill Garner. He was a member of my church in Pine Bluff, Arkansas. Bill was in his seventies. Severe diabetes had left him blind and barely able to get around on the two artificial legs he had as the result of amputations. If anyone had a reason for saying, "I don't have much to offer," it was Bill. No one would have thought of Bill as shirking his responsibilities if he had pointed to his lack of eyesight and mobility and excused himself from any meaningful service.

But Bill Garner would hear nothing of it. Perhaps he couldn't walk door to door, make lengthy speeches, or play on the church softball team, but Bill could dial the phone. Each week he made more than one hundred calls to encourage people who were sick and to invite others to church. A telephone might not seem like much, but it became a powerful tool in Bill Garner's hand.

Robert Tollison was a young deacon at Immanuel Baptist Church in Pine Bluff. During the week, he worked in the parts department of a heating and air conditioning company. He worked long hours, but he didn't have the kind of job that made him rich. When Robert reached into his pockets, there wasn't a great deal of money. But Robert could pull out a large set of keys. Each Sunday Robert arrived early to unlock the many doors at the church. He then spent time making sure the temperature was comfortable in all parts of the facility. Robert would come in the night before a baptism, fill the baptistry, and make sure the water was warm.

Robert never received a standing ovation for his efforts. Few would have known to express their thanks to him for arriving at the church hours before them and staying after they left so the pastor and the church staff could spend more time being attuned to the spiritual needs of the congregation. Robert took what he had—a set of keys and a knowledge of heating and cooling systems—and did a service for people who probably never recognized it.

Pam Burns, a young wife and a mother of two, was a member of Beech Street First Baptist Church of Texarkana, Arkansas. She was faithful in her attendance. Pam was not the type who made a great deal of noise. I don't recall that she sang in the choir or ever stood to be heard during a church business meeting. But she had a very special gift of calligraphy.

During my first political campaign in 1992, the mail would bring a simple white postcard with an encouraging verse of Scripture. Those cards would arrive every day. Each of them was mailed anonymously. The daily Scripture verse became so meaningful and the faithfulness of its delivery so predictable that my wife and I would find ourselves racing to the mailbox to see what word of encouragement awaited us.

It wasn't until months after the campaign had ended that we discovered our secret prayer partner was Pam. She had brought more encouragement and strength to us than she ever could have known. Pam Burns's talent of calligraphy hadn't been known to us, but it wasn't the beauty of her handwriting that brought such hope. It was her faithful expressions of

> *When each of us uses what we have and does it in such a way that other people's lives are touched, it will have a far greater impact than if we had written them a check for one million dollars.*

encouragement for which we will forever be grateful.

Katy Elkins was a college librarian who somehow found time to clip every newspaper article she could find about my first campaign. She compiled several massive scrapbooks that we will always cherish. It's impossible to estimate the number of hours Katy spent gathering, sorting, and pasting the thousands of clips and other items contained in those scrapbooks. The scrapbooks will not be turned into bestsellers, but they hold a priceless value for us.

Frank and Katie Stone are a retired couple whom I came to know at Immanuel Baptist Church in Pine Bluff. Frank wasn't one who liked to speak in front of an audience or even lead in prayer. But he and Katie were excellent cooks. Whenever someone in the church experienced a difficult time such as a death or a serious illness in the family, a dish would appear at their home. Others could be called on to lead in prayer or give speeches. That was fine because Frank and Katie could always be found in the kitchen making something delicious.

What's in your hand? It may be something as simple as a telephone, a set of keys, a ballpoint pen, a bottle of glue, or a cooking utensil. When each of us uses what we have and does it in such a way that other people's lives are touched, it will have a far greater impact than if we had written them a check for one million dollars.

I've known people who have had more than one million dollars, and it made them no happier. In some cases, they wasted it and had nothing to show except expensive appliances that eventually broke, cars that had to be replaced, clothes that went out of style, and large homes that were without love and friendship. But for as long as I live and into the next life, I'll be grateful for those people who shared their talents and did it in such extraordinary ways.

Questions for Reflection and Discussion

1. What does the author mean when he says the disciples of Jesus had a type of "spiritual amnesia"?

2. Do you believe that God equips believers for the experiences they face in life, no matter how difficult they may be? Why or why not?

3. The author gives several examples of people who used their gifts and talents for God's glory. Do you know someone whom you could add to his list of those who maximized their gifts? Take time to thank God for these people and their influence in your life.

143

4. How has God taken inadequate resources, such as he did with the boy's lunch in the feeding of the multitudes, and worked a miracle in your own life?

5. Do you agree with this statement by the author: "We are not called to be successful as much as we're called to be faithful"? Why or why not?

SIXTEEN

No Pain, No Gain

The chipper, young physical therapist exclaimed, "No pain, no gain." She was putting my right leg through contortions. This was to help my knee recover from surgery after my 1984 automobile accident.

I was simply trying to help her in making some "gain." For some reason, she seemed to think I would be greatly encouraged every time she put my leg through a movement that caused a primal scream. On several occasions when she grabbed my leg, hoisted it into the air and told me, "Lift it this way!" I responded, "If I could lift my leg that way, I wouldn't need physical therapy."

I finally was released from physical therapy, but I always remember her motto: "No pain, no gain."

Americans buy aspirin by the millions to relieve our aches and pains. If withstanding the pain represented gain, most Americans would be deep in the hole.

There's simply no painless way to live and succeed. Let's face it. Some things in life aren't pleasant. Even a hard-core optimist would struggle to find something pleasant in circumstances such as the death of a child, the loss of a good job, or the sudden failure of a marriage. Some of the most important parts of our personal character are forged during our "time in the furnace" when impurities are burned away. We're fashioned through life's hurts. They help us understand the difference between our pleasures and our treasures.

Good from Bad

There's simply no painless way to live and succeed.

One of the most misquoted verses in the Bible is Romans 8:28: "And we know that in all things God works for the good of those who love him, who have been called according to his purpose."

Let's be clear—the Bible never said "all things are good." Frankly, some things are bad. When a drunk driver crosses the centerline, runs into an oncoming car and kills a husband, wife, and child, that's not good. When a thirty-three-year-old mother of two young children dies of breast cancer, that's not good. When a faithful husband discovers his wife is cheating on him, that's not good. When a six-year-old is abducted from her backyard while playing and her mutilated body is found several days later in a drainage ditch, that's not good.

146

Those who love God need not stretch their faith to validate Romans 8:28. The Bible doesn't say all things are good. The Bible does say all things "work together for the good." But even then we must qualify the statement by noting that things only work together for the good of those who "love God and are called according to his purpose."

How can all things work together for good when so many things oppose the good? Let me try to explain.

When my wife Janet and I moved to Fort Worth, Texas, for me to attend graduate school in January 1976, we struggled financially as most couples do in similar circumstances. Our struggle intensified when Janet became pregnant. We lost her income but gained the expenses of a baby. We had to make do on the little bit of money I earned. For almost six months, our daily meals consisted of peanut butter and jelly sandwiches and alternating flavors of canned soup.

On the advice of one of our friends, Janet enrolled in a cake decorating course at J. C. Penney with the hope she could decorate cakes to earn a little extra money. Before she could actually make the cakes, she had to invest in several pans and the "squeeze bags" through which the frosting would be applied to the cakes. (A word of advice to husbands: If your wife tells you she's going to decorate cakes to earn some extra income, do yourself a favor and don't let it happen.) Though Janet turned out to be a formidable cake decorator, we nearly went broke "making extra money." After working hard on an elaborate cake, she announced to me, "This is for Glenda's birthday and since we can't afford to get her a present, I'm going to let the cake be my gift." I knew of the hours of work that had gone into decorating a cake. I would ask Janet how much she received for a particular cake. Usually I was greeted with the news that the cake was for one of our friends and she simply didn't feel comfortable charging for it.

I did learn a lot about decorating cakes, though. Janet's first step would be gathering the ingredients and arranging them on the kitchen counter. She then would measure, mix, and bake. I would sometimes come in from work and realize she would be unable to prepare dinner for me that evening. Being the considerate husband I was (and hopefully still am!) I would tell her not to worry about dinner. I then would proceed around the kitchen counter and begin to snack on the various ingredients. Sometimes I would take a large kitchen spoon, dip it into a can of Crisco, and eat directly from the can of shortening. I would follow that up by munching on a stick of butter or eating dry cocoa from a box. Those items would then be washed down by drinking from a bottle of vanilla extract. I would sometimes even eat a couple of cups of raw sifted flour. That way I didn't have to wait for the cake.

Actually, I really didn't eat shortening from the can, butter, dry cocoa, flour, or any of the other ingredients. I'm not sure you've ever thought about it, but the individual ingredients of a cake aren't very appealing if eaten by themselves in their raw state. But we don't eat cake by taking the ingredients one by one. The ingredients are measured and brought together using a carefully tested plan called a recipe. They're mixed and then subjected to an extraordinary fit of violence in a device called a mixer. In fact, rather violent words are used to describe its functions—words like whip and beat. After the ingredients have been put through the mixer, the violence intensifies. The freshly mixed bowl of ingredients, which now are unrecognizable from their original condition, is stuffed into an oven that's hot enough to make one's blood boil. The structure changes from a goo to a spongy mass. Then—and only then—is the cake frosted and served for those who want the reward of something sweet and attractive.

> *Not one ingredient that goes into a cake is necessarily desirable by itself.*

Think about it. Not one ingredient that goes into a cake is necessarily desirable by itself. One would not eat raw flour, dry cocoa, or shortening. The cake isn't judged by the individual ingredients but by how they taste after following the recipe. Then and only then should we assess the finished product.

Not every ingredient of life is pleasant. But mixed with the other ingredients, they have the capacity to form lives that are ever closer to the character of Christ. As we attempt to live beyond our lifetime, we need to recognize that some elements of our lives will be unpleasant. But individual components working together with the other components can result in something good.

Responding to Pain

This is a testament of his love, not his cruelty. The pain in our lives is temporary. It will end when our lives end. Suffering is inevitable for a human being. It is not the presence of suffering but our response to it that determines whether we're made better or made bitter.

In the Sermon on the Mount, Jesus reminded us that our pain can drive us to a level of godliness we never would have known otherwise.

"Blessed are the poor in spirit,
for theirs is the kingdom of heaven.
Blessed are those who mourn,
for they shall be comforted.
Blessed are the meek,
for they shall inherit the earth.
Blessed are those who hunger and thirst for
righteousness
for they shall be filled" (Matt. 5:3–6).

At first it would appear to be a contradiction for Jesus to tell us we're happy when we're spiritually drained, when we experience a great loss, when we've had our will broken or when we stand with deep hunger for what is right. But Jesus understood what most Americans don't understand in our quest for pain-free living. If we experience momentary suffering but it makes us more like Christ and less like our selfish selves, then we really are further along on the road to lasting joy. Second Corinthians 4:17 is one of the most challenging verses of the Bible for me: "For our light and momentary troubles are achieving for us an eternal glory that far outweighs them all."

When I developed a kidney stone during a trip to Puerto Rico in 1998, I had to be temporarily hospitalized in a facility where virtually no one spoke English. I then had to be flown home for the removal of the kidney stone. It's hard for me to believe the apostle Paul could have been so callous as to call my experience light and momentary! I was convinced the apostle Paul had never had a kidney stone. Had he experienced it, surely he would have written about an exception in describing human suffering as light and momentary! During that episode, I was probably as close to God as I've ever been. I was really praying to get even closer. I wanted to experience a medical miracle or go right on to glory—which at the moment would have been fine with me. I found out the only thing worse than having a kidney stone is having a kidney stone while being governor. A detailed description of how it was removed was on the front page of the state's newspapers the next morning.

> *The pain in our lives is temporary.*

In the midst of suffering, it's difficult to believe there's anything "light and momentary" about it. But from the perspective of the eternal ecstasy provided

151

by a faith rooted in God's promises, even the worst earthly troubles are indeed minor and temporary.

Some of life's circumstances help bring our stubborn human will under control. They force us to recognize our human weaknesses and vulnerability. Such experiences form the essence of the idea of "blessed are the meek."

Our Strength Under God's Control

This can be compared with domesticating a wild animal. You must harness the raw power and make sure it will follow directions. When our strength is brought under God's control, it doesn't mean we're weak. The Bible never says, "Blessed are the weak." There's a dramatic difference between meekness and weakness. Weakness means we've lost our strength. Meekness means we simply have it under control and can channel it toward achieving useful goals. Physicists have estimated that if the power of a major hurricane could be harnessed, it could supply all the energy used in the United States for six months. Some hurricanes have an energy level equal to exploding ten atomic bombs every second. Because it's unharnessed and uncontrolled energy, the hurricane destroys all that's in its path.

Pain has a way of taming us. Pain can force us to be emptied of our pride and our sense of self-sufficiency. It makes us realize we can go from full speed to a dead stop in an instant.

I don't like pain. I'm not at the point in my life where I welcome it, readily accept it, or consider it my friend. In the midst of a difficult moment, in fact, I may forget everything I'm saying in this chapter. But deep within me is the comforting truth that pain has a purpose. Because of my relationship with Jesus Christ, I can and will endure. Deep down I realize that unpleasant experiences—no matter how unwelcome—will work with other experiences to bring about a deeper character and a greater since of compassion for those around me who hurt in even greater ways. These experiences will make me grateful this life is not the only one I'm going to live.

Without a doubt, the greatest purpose of pain is to make me glad the life I live in the flesh is not the only one I'll live. As I seek to find comforting words to offer a friend whose daughter was murdered, or as I awkwardly try to find a way to encourage a friend whose wife is dying of cancer, I find comfort in knowing that no matter how bad this occasion may be, it will work "together for the good," though it may be in the next life before I fully understand how.

> *"Blessed are the meek, For they shall inherit the earth."*

I pity those who think life consists of nothing more than the life they're now living. The most tragic are those who believe their value as a human being is tied to their net worth and whose sense of self-esteem is linked to how many people know them and like them. It's far better to have an inner confidence that no matter how many life experiences come your way that can be characterized as "bad things," they're only small distractions and diversions as we race toward a life beyond this one. It will be a life in which there will be no tears, no sorrow, no pain, no disease, no hunger, and no death.

We must accept the fact that life isn't always a party with the chips and cheese dip—sometimes, life hurts. Really hurts. But as the sadistic therapist reminded me, "No pain, no gain."

Questions for Reflection and Discussion

1. Why does the author consider Romans 8:28 one of the most misquoted verses in the Bible?

2. Make a list of bad events in your life through which God eventually worked things for good.

3. Identify a sorrow in your life today. Then ask yourself, "Is God using this bad thing to help me become a better person?

4. Why did the apostle Paul consider his sufferings "light and momentary"?

5. Meditate on Jesus' words, "Blessed are the meek." Then ask yourself, "Am I allowing God's discipline to bring my strength under his control?"

PART IV

A Legacy Loved

SEVENTEEN

How Much Will You Leave Behind?

Once there was a man hunting in thick woods. He became tired because he had been walking all day. As he started home, it began to rain. Soon he was cold and wet. Then he came upon a cabin in the woods. There was no one in the cabin, but there was plenty of dry wood on the front porch.

The hunter took some wood and built a fire in the fireplace. The fire burned brightly, and the hunter was soon comfortable. He noticed a sign above the fireplace that read, "Friend, enjoy the comfort of this little cabin. Rest all you want and stay as long as you like. The only cost to you is to leave the woodpile a little higher than when you found it."

Billy Graham once said, "I've never seen a hearse pulling a U-Haul." Perhaps you have heard the story about the funeral of John D. Rockefeller. A bystander edged up to an accountant for Mr. Rockefeller and asked, "Say, just how much did he leave behind?" The accountant replied, "He left it all. He didn't take a thing with him."

We live in an age of consumerism. Many people judge their worth not by how much they've earned but by how much they've spent. One of our state's economic forecasters reports regularly to me on the status of the Arkansas economy. I often hear about consumer confidence levels. This is viewed as an important barometer of the economy's strength.

> *Many people have built their lives around the strength of their personal buying power. Their lives are based not only on their ability to buy things but in the things they buy.*

On more than one occasion, it has occurred to me that many people have built their lives around the strength of their personal buying power. Their lives are based not only on their ability to buy things but in the things they buy. That is tragic.

At the height of the Texas oil boom, a successful oil millionaire decreed that he be buried in his custom Cadillac. An unusually large grave was dug, and the millionaire was propped in the driver's seat. As the car was being lowered into the ground, someone was heard to exclaim, "Man, that's living." Actually, that is not living at all. It is dying. The most expensive casket will not make up for a life that has been lived in spiritual poverty.

Driving down the highway one day, I was startled by a bumper sticker that advertised the utter vanity of the car's owner. The sticker proclaimed, "He who dies with the most toys wins." It is a sad value system that rates a person's worth by the accumulation of things that can wear out, rot, go out of style, or be stolen.

> *The most expensive casket will not make up for a life that has been lived in spiritual poverty.*

Some people preach that having much is a sin, but that is not what the Bible teaches. The issue of wealth is not how much you have but how you got it. The two basic commands regarding accumulating wealth contain a negative and a positive. The negative is not to lay up treasures on earth (Matt. 6:19). The positive is to lay up treasures in heaven (Matt. 6:20). Too many people judge the wealth of others by the property they own or the lifestyle they enjoy.

One of the great challenges of life is determining that our pleasure shouldn't be based on the amount of our treasure. When life and its enjoyment are defined by what we have accumulated, we're to be pitied rather than envied. Our treasure should never become our job, home, car, property, or any other "toys." Consumerism can be intoxicating and addictive. Those who are swept up in its power find their occasional moments of ecstasy tied to the purchase of something. As soon as the pleasure of the purchase subsides, the person already is seeking another value-oriented high.

A young couple from Little Rock announced they were leaving a relatively comfortable upper-middle-class life to become missionaries in Indonesia. They said, "We've fulfilled the American dream, but it didn't fulfill us." Like the heroin addict who is never quite satisfied, a person who gets a rush from the sound of a cash register as it rings up another purchase is one who will never know the simple joy of contentment.

A sense of real peace is achieved only when you can say that material things are genuinely immaterial. It's not so much what we have but what has us that will determine our inner tranquility. Some people have a great deal but are not the least bit enamored by it. Others have precious little but are totally consumed with the obsession to have more. There's no prohibition in God's Word to having much, but there's a strong admonition not to allow even a little to possess us (Matt. 19:22–24).

Some people will end up prosperous even though it was not their goal to lay up great treasure on this earth. It just seems to happen naturally for them. That is not necessarily bad as long as they are responsible stewards of their wealth and share it generously.

All of us, regardless of what we have, are encouraged to store up treasure in heaven where moths can't destroy it and thieves can't steal it (Matt. 6:19–20).

None of us really own anything. We may possess things, but when we die, they will be in the hands of someone else. Ultimately, God owns everything. Our role on this earth is primarily that of a caretaker—or to use the biblical expression, a steward.

If we use what we have for God's glory rather than our own, we most likely are laying up heavenly treasures rather than earthly treasures. Our priority should always be the ultimate result rather than the immediate result. There's a marked difference between spending and investment. That which has lasting value—especially that which has the ability to bring spiritual blessings—is worth far more than those things that depreciate from the moment we buy them until they are thrown away.

A good barometer of the value of our possessions is to ask whether anyone will benefit from our wealth a century from now. If a parent gives a son a new car and fine clothes but fails to give him character, will the son have benefited in the long term?

My own parents never knew earthly wealth. Both grew up poor and were precluded from anything

> *If we use what we have for God's glory rather than our own, we most likely are laying up heavenly treasures rather than earthly treasures.*

more than a high school education because of World
War II and the necessity of supporting their family. By
most earthly standards, their accumulations were
meager. But what they did have was paid for in full
and earned by the sweat of their brow.

On December 31, 1991, I announced to my congregation at Beech Street First Baptist Church in
Texarkana, Arkansas, that I would resign as pastor in
order to seek public office. I had told my parents of
my intentions. My mother wrote me a letter dated
December 30, 1991. Five days after writing the letter,
she suffered a ruptured aneurysm in her brain. She
lived until September 30, 1999, but she was never the
same mentally or physically.

Her letter to me was read at her funeral. It is a precious reminder of what real treasure is all about. Her
letter indicates that my inheritance is far more valuable than it would have been if she had left a portfo-
lio worth millions of dollars.

> Dear Mike,
> We realize that we do not have a
> gift with words or the gift of saying
> the right thing at the right time, but
> we do want to say a few words at
> this time. Of course you realize that
> this is your earthly mother and father
> speaking and not your Heavenly
> Father speaking.
> When you were given to us by our
> Heavenly Father, we certainly were

not acquainted with God's Holy
Spirit, so we tried the best we knew
how to bring you and Pat up to do
what was right, to know when things
were right and to know when they
were wrong, to do unto others as you
would have them do unto you, be
humble in all that you do and to say
please and thank you, yes sir, yes
ma'am, no sir, no ma'am, speak to
everyone, call them by name, respect
other people, and do what you could
for those less fortunate than yourself.

We are so very very thankful to
God for what you both have turned
out to be, and we always thank God
in our prayers for this.

Now that you both are grown up,
married, and are parents yourselves,
we have tried hard not to tell you
what to do with yourselves, etc. . .
(even though it is hard sometimes),
and it is because of this that we have
not interfered with any of your decisions. Instead we will swallow real
hard and pray very much that God
will help you both in everything you
do.

To make a long story a little
shorter, we love you both so very
much, ask for your forgiveness
wherein we have failed you, and

shall continue to pray that you both
will always seek and do God's will.
With much love,
Mom

Jesus reminds us we can only have one master.
We'll either serve the spiritual or the temporal (Luke
16:13). As inhabitants of planet Earth, we're involved
in the world and its possessions. But we don't have
to be obsessed with those possessions. After all, we're
just passing through. One of the challenges of life is
to determine whether our responsibilities to God are more important
than fulfilling our desires.

> *As inhabitants of planet earth, we're involved in the world and its possessions. But we don't have to be obsessed with those possessions.*

A little boy was given two quarters. One was to be placed in the offering plate at church, and the other was for ice cream. As he walked along holding the quarters, he dropped one. As it rolled away, the little boy said, "Sorry, God, there went your quarter."

I once worked for James Robison, whose world outreach has spanned decades through evangelism, encouragement, and feeding hungry children. James once received a letter from a father in Arkansas following an outdoor crusade in that area. In the letter, the father related how his daughter had started attending church at age six because the church had a bus route near their home. The little girl begged her daddy each Sunday to go to church with her, but he would tell her he was too busy running his gas station. He said he had to work on Sunday to make sure they had plenty of money.

For several years the little girl faithfully attended church and urged her father to go with her. Each Sunday he offered the same excuse. The girl finally stopped going to church. That provided a certain relief for the father, since he would no longer have to repeat his excuse.

A few years later the man received a phone call and was summoned to the school his daughter attended. The daughter, now twelve years old, had been sitting in a car with several other students sniffing aerosol spray from a bag for the temporary high it gave them. That morning's high took her higher than she had ever been—to her death. An autopsy showed the girl was pregnant.

> *It's certain that we'll leave everything in this world behind. What is important is what we send on ahead.*

The final words of the father's letter were the most haunting: "James, please tell daddies not to live for material things while forgetting the spiritual."

It's certain that we'll leave everything in this world behind. What is important is what we send on ahead.

Questions for Reflection and Discussion

1. What are the negative and positive commands that Jesus gave regarding the accumulation of wealth?

2. Why does consumerism become intoxicating and addictive for some people?

3. What's the difference between owning things and letting the things we have own us?

4. Describe the specific values we should pass on to our children that are more important than a financial legacy.

5. How can a person lay up "heavenly treasures" rather than "earthly treasures"?

EIGHTEEN

The Follow Factor

I'm an avid duck hunter, and I live in a great place for it. Arkansas has some of the best duck hunting in North America. I do my best to experience as many days as possible hunting alongside my faithful Labrador retriever, Jet.

Being in the great outdoors at sunrise and watching the splendor of waterfowl answer the sound of the duck call is the second greatest part of the hunt. The greatest pleasure is watching my dog retrieve. The third pleasure is the fellowship shared with others in the duck blind. As strange as it may seem to nonhunters, the least important aspect is pulling the trigger on the shotgun.

During duck season, I enjoy watching all kinds of waterfowl make their way down the Mississippi flyway as they migrate from Canada to Mexico. I've long been fascinated by the geese that fly in a V formation. Experiments in a wind tunnel showed what happens in a V formation. Each goose creates an upward lift

We don't live in a vacuum. Someone is likely following in our footsteps in the same way we're following others.

for the goose behind. The formation gives almost 70 percent more flying range than if a goose flies alone. Researchers also discovered that when one of the geese gets behind, the others honk encouragement for it to keep up.

Like waterfowl that have an instinct to fly south in the winter, there is something intuitive that causes us to look toward our future. We think in terms of what will be remembered of our lives and whether anything of significance will remain once we're gone.

The kind of leader we'll be is tied directly to what kind of follower we were for those who blazed the trail before us. We don't live in a vacuum. Someone is likely following in our footsteps in the same way we're following others.

I've traveled to Israel nine times. One of my favorite places is Masada, the ancient Roman fortress in the desert near the Dead Sea where about nine hundred men, women, and children took refuge and held off an entire Roman army for almost three years. The fall of Masada in A.D. 73 marked the end of a Jewish state until 1948, when Israel was reborn. The extraordinary history behind Masada and the captivating story of those final moments, when the Jews chose to die rather than subject themselves to Roman slavery, makes it one of the most interesting places in the world to visit.

My first trip to Masada was one I'll long remember. Prior to going, I had read all I could about it so I would be prepared for my pilgrimage to this special place. When we arrived at the flat-topped fortress in the desert, I saw a cable car that stretched from the base of the mountain to a landing area near the top of Masada. My heart sank. Since that time, I've overcome what was extreme acrophobia and now routinely ride in helicopters. I've even experienced a memorable ride in a hot-air balloon. On that first trip to Masada, though, my sense of adventure was far from developed.

The thought of getting into that cable car scared me. I tried to hide my fear, but sweat poured from my head, my hands were clammy, my heart was beating too fast, and my breath was shallow and rapid. Most people would have thought nothing of it. But for me the thought of being suspended above nothing but rock was terrifying beyond description. I tried to talk my way out of the line.

As we approached the point of boarding the cable car, I was nearing nausea. Just then, I noticed a large group of Catholic nuns getting ready to board. There wasn't a hint of anxiety among them. In fact, they were laughing and acting as casually as if they were being seated for dinner. Perhaps it was my pride that took hold, but I thought to myself, "If those Catholic sisters aren't afraid, neither should I be." I took a deep breath, boarded the cable car, and lived to tell about it. I've returned many times, and I've never again been afraid.

As I reflected on that experience and others like it, I was reminded that sometimes our desire to do something overwhelms our fear of doing it. One of the ways we challenge our fears is to recognize we're not being asked to do something for the first time. We must realize that others have taken similar steps and are alive and well.

It's natural to fear death. If we sat for long periods contemplating nothing but death, we would soon become neurotic. There's something disturbing about moving toward a destination we've never seen in order to spend eternity with many people we've never met.

Overcoming the fear of death involves recognizing we're not migrating alone. Like geese, we're part of a large family traveling in the same direction. One of the reasons we're commanded to congregate in mutual fellowship (Heb. 10:25) is so we can gain strength from those with whom we fly. They, in turn, can gain strength from us.

There's genuine efficiency achieved as we face our future with fellow travelers. When we're weary and lag behind, the encouragement of others becomes like the honking of the geese, cheering us on toward the next step, the next day, the next challenge.

We're able to face death more comfortably knowing that many people have gone before us. While we're not exactly sure what our journey will be like, we know it's a well-worn path. For Christian believers, there's a sense that the one in whom our entire faith is focused has not only traveled through the valley of death but has returned to announce his victory over it. His invitation is for us to join him in the same journey.

We may have never passed this way before, but it doesn't mean the route is untested. Believing we will live beyond our lifetime is an incredibly liberating factor. It translates into a zest for living and certain ambivalence about dying.

Moving toward death isn't something any of us enjoy talking about. But for those who are confident the destination is worth the process, it holds a certain sense of adventure. I've spent countless hours flying in small airplanes, often in less-than-ideal weather. One thing I've come to appreciate is the skill of a pilot who can successfully guide an aircraft through the most rugged instrument-flying conditions.

> *We're able to face death more comfortably knowing that many people have gone before us. While we're not exactly sure what our journey will be like, we know it's a well-worn path.*

One thing is for certain in such a situation: The pilot cannot act according to what he thinks or what he feels. He must fly the airplane by relying on the instruments to tell him if he is up or down. He puts his complete trust in those instruments. Flight instructors often say, "A pilot who begins to trust his feelings rather than his instruments is already dead. What's left to be determined is the exact spot of the crash."

The Old Testament tells how God's people spent forty years in the wilderness (see Num. 13–14). They were told to follow a pair of clouds and later the ark of the covenant. They didn't know where they were or where they were going, but they were instructed to keep their eyes fixed on the ark and follow by faith.

One of the important lessons from this event is that God doesn't tell us to head out in the direction of our choice and do the best we can while he tags along to pick up the pieces. He goes ahead of us, inviting us to stay close and follow while ensuring us of a safe arrival. If we focus on the fact that we have

God doesn't tell us to head out in the direction of our choice and do the best we can while he tags along to pick up the pieces. He goes ahead of us, inviting us to stay close and follow while ensuring us of a safe arrival.

not ventured though death's door, we'll be overwhelmed with the sense of dread. But if we keep our faith fixed on the God ahead of us, who has traveled this way before, our steps will be firm, although we still might have moments of anxiety.

In the pilgrimage of our life, it isn't necessary that we bring our plans to God for his approval. Our task is to accept and follow the plans he already has drawn out. A person who brings detailed plans to an architect, a recipe to a chef, or tools to a mechanic is one who already has rejected the expertise of the person he approaches. As we move toward the conclusion of our lives and the certainty of our death, we should not be so foolish as to tell God what it will be like. We must allow God to chart and steer our course.

In February 2000, I joined six governors at a meeting in Salt Lake City. We went to Winter Park, site of the 2002 Winter Olympics. The governors were invited to take a crash course (no pun intended) in bobsled driving and then steer a bobsled down the Olympic course. Having grown up in Arkansas, I had never seen a bobsled, much less had the opportunity to drive one. Mental pictures of the bobsled under my command flying off the course and down a steep mountain had my stomach in knots.

I could barely sleep the night before. I woke up at 4:30 A.M., plugged my laptop computer into the hotel phone system, made an Internet connection, and spent two-and-a-half hours reading everything I could about bobsleds. I went into the experience with much greater knowledge but no less fear.

Once again it was not a sudden surge of courage that caused me to get seated (awkwardly, I might add) in the bobsled and put my faith in the sixteen-year-old athlete who was my push-off man. It was the presence of dozens of television camera crews, newspaper photographers, and spectators. That's what caused me to consent to being pushed down an icy track carved along the mountainside, reaching speeds of more than sixty miles per hour, and experiencing four Gs of pull as we made the turns.

No, it was not courage. It was the fact that two governors already had made their bobsled trips before me. Word had filtered back that both had survived. And there were so many people looking on. I knew that even if I was killed doing it, I would go out in a blaze of glory. If I backed out now, I would have a hard time facing my fellow governors again. The trip in the bobsled turned out to be the experience of a lifetime. It's one I'll forever cherish, though not likely repeat.

One day I'll face death. I believe I'll pass through it successfully, not because I've overcome all my fears but because I'm confident of a God who has gone before me and made the journey successfully. And because I'm being cheered on toward the finish line by those around me.

Questions for Reflection and Discussion

1. The author describes how he overcame his acrophobia—extreme fear of heights. Is there some irrational fear in your own life? What do you need to do to overcome it?

2. What does the author mean by this statement: "Overcoming the fear of death involves recognizing we're not migrating alone"?

3. How has Jesus made it easier for his followers to face the inevitability of their own deaths?

4. God has not chosen to tell us everything we might like to know about death and the life beyond. Can you think of any possible reasons why he has not given us perfect knowledge about these matters?

5. What are some certainties that believers can count on as they think about death and the life beyond?

NINETEEN

Toward the Exit Sign

"There are only two certainties in life—death and taxes." This statement is often repeated, but it is only half true—considering the number of people sent to jail for not paying their taxes. It's inaccurate to say that everyone pays taxes. But it's certain we'll all die sooner or later, ready or not.

Some will leave this life rather naturally, much like those who shuffle toward the door at the end of the movie once the lights are turned on. Even though the seats are comfortable, there's really no reason to continue sitting there. Others may find the exit to be like that of the person who wishes to go one way but is forced to go another by the overwhelming force of the crowd as it leaves the theater. Still others may leave long before the movie has ended. No matter how we go, death is certain.

Let's not be mistaken. Death is not our friend. It's a bitter enemy. Death takes a baby out of a mother's

> *Though cus-toms may have changed, the fact that all of us will die has not changed.*

arms. It removes the voice of a father who speaks words of guidance and encouragement to his children. Death leaves an empty chair at the dinner table and stills the laughter at family gatherings. It causes people to regret the things they did and the things they failed to do as they stand over the coffin of a loved one.

The ways we deal with death have changed, even in my lifetime. I can remember the old Southern custom of "sitting up." Friends and relatives would take turns literally sitting with the body from the time of death until the time of burial. I can recall another tradition of having the body in the home rather than the funeral parlor. Years ago, it wasn't uncommon for people to go to the hospital to get well but come home to die.

The custom of "sitting up" is almost a thing of the past, and I don't recall a body being taken to a home in years. Through organizations such as hospices, though, many people are returning to the idea that it's better to die in your home while comforted by family and friends. While customs may have changed, the fact that all of us will die has not changed.

In the past several years, we've attempted to bring some dignity back to the process. It's hard to die with dignity in a hospital environment while surrounded by IVs, catheters, and respirators. There's the noise from the hospital corridors and the interruptions of the hospital staff being summoned to various locations.

Most of us don't have the luxury—if you can call it that—of knowing the time, date, place, and circumstances of our death. It might happen suddenly with an accident or a heart attack. It might be a protracted process such as cancer. But there are some things we can and should know about death.

Death Is a Certainty for Everyone

The Bible teaches, "Man is destined to die once, and after that to face judgment" (Heb. 9:27). We live our lives as a series of appointments. My schedule is the most complicated aspect of my life. Several people work to fill virtually every hour of my day with meetings, speeches, and appointments. I'm amused when someone comes up to me and asks, "What are you doing on April 3?" Little do they know that I'm barely able to keep up with what I'll do tomorrow. Living with a busy schedule is the greatest challenge of being a governor.

But I've learned that the appointments on my calendar can be rescheduled when necessary. A tornado sweeping through the state, killing and injuring people and destroying millions of dollars worth of property, will suddenly change the schedule. The important gives way to the urgent as every appointment is evaluated. Most of us are used to rescheduling appointments.

The one appointment beyond rescheduling is our appointment with death. Death occurs to good people and bad people, to the faithful and the unfaithful. Death is inevitable whether we're rich or poor. Our religion may give us comfort as we approach death, but it will not change its inevitability. Death is the ultimate equalizer and the grim reminder that no matter how healthy, wealthy, or important we are, we're not invincible. We will die.

Death Is Determined by God

God has the key of life and death. "I am the Living One; I was dead, and behold I am alive for ever and ever! And I hold the keys of death and Hades" (Rev. 1:18). We're reminded that we enter this life on our way out. Job 14:5 says, "Man's days are determined; you have decreed the number of his months and have set limits he cannot exceed."

All of us know people who should have lived but died. We also know people who should have died but lived. I remember being stunned by the death of fellow students when I was a teenager. Somehow it seemed impossible that someone my age could die.

I recall a classmate who was recovering from a motorcycle accident with what seemed to be no more than a broken bone. A blood clot formed, dislodged, and killed him. It didn't seem real, but the grief of his family and friends was very real.

A high school classmate had barely started college when her date lost control of a car, slid off the road, and hit a tree. He walked away from the accident, but she was killed instantly. I'll never forget the funeral as hundreds of friends from high school and college tried to understand how a person so young, beautiful, and vibrant could be laughing and living one moment and be gone the next.

Technology has extended the lives of thousands who a few years ago would have died. But while the advancement of technology can change the outlook for the immediate, it cannot change the ultimate.

Death Ends Human Responsibility

When a person dies, one can do no more for that person or to that person, although many attempt to continue a relationship that can no longer exist. In the Bible, even Saul tried to talk to the dead (1 Sam. 28:7–15). Many still do. Others simply deny the death of a loved one has occurred.

One of the most difficult parts of the grief process is to accept the reality of death and the transition from a time of mourning to a time of reentry into life.

> *Death is the ultimate equalizer and the grim reminder that no matter how healthy, wealthy, or important we are, we're not invincible. We will die.*

In 2 Samuel, one can read about the extraordinary grief experienced by King David following the death of his son. But David was encouraged as he realized the time for mourning had ended and it was time to accept responsibility for the living (see 2 Sam. 12:15–23).

> *One of the most difficult parts of the grief process is to accept the reality of death and the transition from a time of mourning to a time of reentry into life.*

After a death, there are many practical things that must be confronted. We must deal with funeral arrangements, disposing of the person's personal items, tying up loose ends, and going through what seems to be an endless pile of paperwork dealing with insurance, Social Security, and estate matters. As loved ones move beyond the death of a relative or friend, the vacuum left by the death can create a great level of discomfort.

Some people's lives become empty since their days had been filled with activities related to the deceased. The routine of caring for a person can become so ingrained that the caregiver doesn't realize how many hours each day were being spent on the task. The caregiver suddenly has a lot of time on his or her hands. The lack of something to do creates anxiety and sometimes even guilt.

One of the world's most comprehensive researchers on the subject of death is Dr. Elisabeth Kubler-Ross. In her classic work *2*, she describes the five stages of death and grief. They are denial, anger, bargaining, grieving, and acceptance. Dr. Kubler-Ross found that even though the stages may come in different degrees and in a different order for different people, each stage will be a part of the process.

At some point, we want to deny that a relative or friend is actually dying. There will be anger— perhaps at God, perhaps at medical personnel, or perhaps at the drunk driver who killed our loved one. It's not unusual that a person will engage in a period of bargaining: "God, if you let my loved one live, I'll be more faithful and will forgive all the people who have wronged me." Grieving grows out of the natural sense of sorrow and hurt.

Finally, although it may take years for some people, there's a sense of acceptance. That's not to say we're content with the death. Acceptance may not mean that things return to normal. It simply means we've faced the reality that the loved one isn't coming back and that we must go on with our own lives.

Someone observed that death is as irrevocable as a haircut. Death actually is much more irrevocable since the hair grows back and we have another opportunity to style it, color it, or cut it.

Death Displays God's Judgment

We don't necessarily die because of a specific sin for which God punishes us. But there's a sense in which all death is the result of universal sin in our world and in our lives. If there had been no sin, there would be no death. But because there is universal sin, there will be universal death. Some people believe each death is the direct result of God's getting angry or getting even with someone. This view is not only far from the biblical teaching, it's just plain cruel. None of us can know for certain why another person died.

Perhaps the most insensitive thing I've ever seen was when a misguided friend said to the parents of a child who had just died, "You need to pray and find out what you did to make God take your child from you."

Some deaths, according to Hebrews, occur because the deceased is simply too good to go on in this world (Heb. 11:37–38). Death is, in fact, a reward for a life well lived.

During my time as a pastor in Pine Bluff, my children were very small. One Sunday night after church, a couple invited us to their home for refreshments. They were older and had not had children in their home for years.

On the way to their home, my wife and I instructed our three children, whose ages ranged from three to nine, to be on their best behavior. We told them not to touch anything or pick anything up.

184

We further instructed them that they were to sit politely and behave. They weren't to eat or drink anything that could easily be spilled. Like little angels, each of them said they understood.

As we walked through the front door of the nicely appointed home, I was shocked to see that not only was the home decorated with delicate treasures on each shelf and table but that there also was a lush white carpet. I suddenly told the children they were not hungry or thirsty, their hands needed to remain in their pockets, and they were not to touch anything.

Somehow the halos on my children turned into horns. Soon, they were trotting off with the man and lady of the house, asking questions about the treasures on the shelves and occasionally picking up items. The problem was there were three of them and only two of us as parents.

Things got worse when the lady of the house announced she wanted to serve us hot fudge sundaes. The thought of my three children dropping hot fudge on that white carpet caused me to lose any desire for ice cream. One by one, I took my children down the hall to the restroom despite their loud insistence they didn't need to go. The purpose of the trip was to make sure they understood our agreement not to touch anything, eat anything, or drink anything.

I'm sure they meant well, but by the time they were back down the hall the promises were forgotten. The things on the shelves were too much to

> *There's no greater hope in all the human heart than to know that the inevitability of death is met with the assurance that life doesn't end.*

resist. So was the allure of ice cream dripping with hot fudge.

I became convinced I wouldn't be able to get my kids to keep their promise of a hands-off policy, and there was no way I could be assured the beautiful white carpet could be kept from having a coating of hot fudge. It was at that point I gave my wife what every couple understands. I gave her "the look."

You know what I mean. It's that unspoken communication that causes a mother to look at her watch, smile, and graciously say, "My, I didn't realize how late it is. As much as we would love to stay, we really need to get home and put the kids to bed. But we certainly enjoyed being here." We gathered the children up and left in order to spare ourselves embarrassment.

In some ways, there may be times when our heavenly Father takes someone home earlier than expected in order to protect his good name and to spare our earthly environment from any additional destructive behavior on that person's part. One thing is certain: Only he knows when those times are. Even then, he does it for our good as well as his. It's certainly not something we should speculate about.

Death Is Different for Believers

During my tenure as a pastor, I presided at almost four hundred funerals. I concluded that while believers don't escape death, they do overcome it. One of the most powerful sermons I've heard regarding death and the preparation for it was titled "Born Once—Die Twice, Born Twice—Die Once." The greatest hope we have is that we have life that is eternal. Our faith as Christians is grounded in the belief that Jesus Christ not only died but rose from the grave.

We might say, "I'm going to fly to New York." We don't actually do the flying. The airplane does. But because we are in the airplane, we go wherever it goes. This is what it means to be "in Christ." It isn't that we have the power to overcome death and have everlasting life. But he overcame death and has eternal life. If we're in him, we share in his destination.

There's no greater hope in all the human heart than to know that the inevitability of death is met with the assurance that life doesn't end. The Bible makes clear that our life beyond death is one in which there are no headlines, no hospitals, no hurts, no hardships, no heat waves, no heart attacks, no homelessness, no hunger, no humiliations, and no hell.

Not only is the destination decidedly different; facing death is remarkably different for believers. The custom at most funerals is that after the memorial service, the family is given a few moments for one last viewing of the body before the trip to the cemetery. In the hundreds of funerals I conducted, I could hear a kind of weeping in those families where faith abounded that was different from those families where faith was absent.

In each case, the grief was real, and the tears were genuine. But those who had faith cried with a loss that sounded as if it at least had a bottom. Those who believed death ended all relationships and that nothing existed afterward cried with a sense of emptiness and abandonment that was haunting.

This type of weeping went beyond mere crying. It was what the Scriptures described as "weeping and gnashing of teeth" (Matt. 25:30). It was a gut-wrenching sense of grief that had no bottom. It was a grief that sounded as if it were coming from a pit without a floor. It was chilling to the bone.

Death Divides God's Treasures

The Bible teaches that we're judged. It's not that we're judged as to whether we'll have eternal life. That's determined by our faith rather than our works. But neither heaven nor hell is a place of equals.

Revelation 20:12–13 says, "And I saw the dead, great and small, standing before the throne, and books were opened. Another book was opened, which is the book of life. The dead were judged according to what they had done as recorded in the books. The sea gave up the dead that were in it, and death and Hades gave up the dead that were in them, and each person was judged according to what he had done."

Clearly, there are rewards based on the manner in which we lived our lives. In the same way, the Scriptures teach that hell is not the same, though it could be argued there's no part of it that could be comfortable enough to be called tolerable. It starts bad and only gets worse. Hell for child molesters and serial killers is most likely even more intense than for the person who out of sheer spiritual rebellion rejected God's hope.

> *When we think about how temporary our possessions are, it makes the things we do to accumulate them seem silly and meaningless.*

Death Destroys Human Accomplishment

No matter what we think we've done and how well we've done it, it's certain that at the moment of our death our independence comes to a halt. The great and mighty are equally as dead as the lowly and poor. We come into the world without possessions, and we leave without possessions.

Many stores have installed devices so a person trying to exit with unpurchased merchandise triggers an alarm. Death is an even more effective alarm system. No matter what we have accumulated in this life, we'll leave it at the door when we reach the exit.

When we think about how temporary our possessions are, it makes the things we do to accumulate them seem silly and meaningless.

It's easy to envy those people who have nicer cars, expensive homes, more fashionable clothes, and the other trappings of worldly success. There's nothing wrong with possessing things, but there's something tragic about being possessed by those things. No matter how much wealth and power we attain, those possessions and power depart the moment we draw our final breath.

We cannot stop the process of death. The best doctors and the best medicine can only slow it down. We can't prevent it, but we can prepare for it. In the Gospel of John, Jesus tells us not to be troubled or afraid. He gives us a wonderful promise: "I go and prepare a place for you" (John 14:3).

Questions for Reflection and Discussion

1. Why are we shocked and puzzled by the death of children and youth?

2. Why do some people attempt to communicate with the dead?

3. Name and describe the five stages of death and grief.

4. Do you agree with this statement by the author: "There's a sense in which all death is the result of universal sin in our world and in our lives"? Why or why not?

5. Have you ever known a person who refused to accept the fact that a loved one had died? What behavior did this person demonstrate?

6. What hope do Christians have that makes facing death different for them than it is for non-Christians?

TWENTY

The Legacy of Your Loot

Most Americans will tell you money might not guarantee happiness, but it sure helps. Few subjects bring stronger reactions than the topic of money. Friendships are lost because of it. Marriages are destroyed because of it. Churches split over the spending of it. Political campaigns are fought over how it's received and spent.

One of the most commonly misinterpreted verses in the Bible is about money. Many people will tell you the Bible says money is the root of all evil. The Bible never says money is the root of all evil. It says "the love of money is a root of all kinds of evil" (1 Tim. 6:10). There are two kinds of people in the world: those who admit they are affected by money or the lack thereof and those who lie and say they're not affected.

Not everyone has a love of money, but all of us have the need for enough of it so we can feed our families, put gasoline in our cars, put a roof over our heads, and put clothing on our backs. Some people who have much wealth love money less than those who have little. Net worth is not an indication of a healthy relationship with personal wealth.

While the most important legacy we leave is our character, this chapter presents five basic principles of leaving the right kind of legacy with our loot.

We Should Provide Honest Resources for Our Family

Since the time of Adam, hard work has been a spiritual as well as a practical requirement for honest wages. Proverbs 10:4 says, "Lazy hands make a man poor, but diligent hands bring wealth."

Few things hurt a person's testimony of faith more than being irresponsible with debts to others.

The rapid growth of various forms of gambling in our culture has fueled the notion that it's possible to get something for nothing. But wagering will never produce wealth in a manner as predictable as work. If the vice of making the bet were as valid as the virtue of getting a job, few people would invest their resources in the stock market or use their money to start companies. The truly wealthy people I know don't take their money to casinos or buy lottery tickets.

After tiring of the grumbling of an extremely wealthy man, a man of modest means said, "I have very little. You have millions. But actually I'm richer than you because I have as much as I need or want. Sadly, you don't."

While we read of an occasional person who falls into money, most of us don't suddenly become rich. There are rare exceptions—such as the couple whose sewer lines collapsed. As they dug, the man found a few gold coins and then some more. He ended up discovering coins worth more than $1 million. The coins were left over from the gold rush days of 1849. The likelihood of that happening for most of us is about the same as winning a multimillion-dollar sweepstakes.

Perhaps you heard about the person who was excited when he was told he had just won three million dollars in a sweepstakes. He lost his enthusiasm when he was informed he would receive one dollar a year for the next three million years.

We Should Pay Debt Promptly

The Bible speaks of debt as a trap and those who are taken captive by debt as slaves (Prov. 6:1–5). Americans are certainly adept at borrowing money. There is the story of an immigrant who came to this country without a dime but in less than a year owed $400 million! Yes, Americans believe in borrowing.

Some Christians believe you should never borrow money under any circumstance. The Bible teaches that we should pay what we owe and not obligate ourselves for what we cannot pay. The prohibition is thus against failing to pay off debt and accumulating debts that are beyond our capacity to pay back in a reasonable amount of time. Few things hurt a person's testimony of faith more than being irresponsible with debts to others.

A scoundrel in the community became very religious. A friend said, "I hear you're starting to attend church. I guess that means you'll be giving up drinking, smoking, and cussing. Does that also mean you're going to be paying off your debts?" The newly converted scoundrel replied, "Wait a minute. That's not religion; that's business."

As difficult as it is to leave a positive legacy, it's not difficult to leave a negative legacy by failing to pay debts or, even worse, leaving heirs with the burden of paying them. We certainly shouldn't be like the ambitious young man who ran up debts all over town. One of the merchants to whom he owed a considerable sum approached him one day and said, "Look, I've about had it waiting for you to pay me. I need my money this week."

The young man replied, "Please don't talk to me so harshly. If you do, I'll take your name out of the hat."

The merchant asked what he meant.

The young man said, "Each month, I take all the bills I receive and put them in a large hat. I draw from the hat and pay the bills until I run out of money. Then I put all the other bills in the hat and leave them there until the next month's drawing."

When the merchant complained that such a procedure was unacceptable, the young man repeated, "If you're going to be that way about it, I'll quit putting your bills in the hat."

We Should Plan Our Purchases Carefully

Another principle of sound financial management is to avoid impulse buying. Most of the time we buy things that have no lasting value. One of the challenges of being an American when the economy is good is to be honest with ourselves when it comes to buying what we need rather than what we want. We should be responsible stewards when it comes to managing what we have. We should do our best to shop for the best prices and wait for sales. This enables us to leave more for rainy days and to preserve a financial legacy for our children and grandchildren.

Only through giving do we learn to have an unselfish spirit.

John Wanamaker, a successful businessman in the nineteenth century, bought his first Bible at age eleven. Later in life, he said, "I've made purchases involving millions of dollars, but the little Bible I bought for $2.75 was my best investment ever. It was the foundation of my life."

Leaving the right kind of legacy involves not only leaving things behind but also passing on a lifestyle that will allow our children to remain debt free.

We Should Protect Our Assets Diligently

It's wrong to hoard things, but it's equally wrong to fail to protect our assets. Being able to take care of our possessions not only indicates our trustworthiness with God but also teaches our children how to manage money and material things.

> *The true believer realizes that whatever money or material possessions he or she has, are temporary.*

A beggar approached a pedestrian and said, "Give me a dollar." The pedestrian replied, "I might give you a dime or a quarter, but I'm not giving you a dollar." The beggar said indignantly, "Hey, you can give me a dollar or not, but don't tell me how to run my business." Being a good manager of the resources God has entrusted us with involves insuring what we can't afford to replace. We should also make long-range financial plans and invest the money we don't need for current expenses for the future.

We Should Practice Unselfish Giving Cheerfully

Because of the proliferation of sermons on the subject of giving, it's one of the most often preached about but least often practiced elements of life.

We don't give to bail "poor ol' God" out of trouble. The reason a person of faith gives isn't because the recipient has a need to receive but because the giver has a need to give. Only through giving do we learn to have an unselfish spirit. The people who are willing to end friendships over financial issues are the ones for whom money is a god.

We shouldn't be concerned about how others make or spend their money as long as it is honest. But those whose hearts are greedy, whose spirits are selfish, and who covet what others have are quick to criticize and condemn others for what they possess, how they received it, and what they do with it. The quickest way to discover who has an unhealthy love for money is to talk about the good fortune of someone who came into an unexpected treasure. The person who expresses resentment about this is probably the one possessed by the love of money.

If we're under grace, we should learn the art of joyful giving—not what we're required to give but what we're inspired to give.

The true believer realizes that whatever money or material possessions he or she has are temporary. Such a person is not so much enamored with God's gifts as he is enamored with the God who has given the gifts. We're admonished in the Bible to honor God with the firstfruits of our lives (Exod. 34:26). This is a way to prove we trust him, not merely by saying the words but by living out the deeds.

The most wonderful giving in the world is giving that cannot be repaid. Giving to those who will give back isn't really giving. It's trading. True spiritual giving involves an extraordinary level of faith. God's giving is motivated by his character, not by his desire to receive a return favor for the gift.

A reporter traveling to write articles on mission work came upon a missionary who was treating the sores of lepers. The reporter said, "I wouldn't do that for a million dollars." The missionary replied, "Neither would I. But I'm more than happy to do it in service to my Savior."

A greedy spirit often manifests itself when a person has the opportunity to give unselfishly. A man who started with practically nothing committed to give a percentage of his income to God. The first week the man needed to give less than $10 because his income didn't reach $100. As time passed, his business prospered. Soon, he was giving almost $1,000 a week.

The now successful businessman went back to his pastor and said, "I stated that if God would bless me I would give him a percentage, but I didn't know my business would do as well as it has done. How can I get released from that promise?"

The pastor thought for a moment and said, "I don't think you can be released from your promise, but why don't we get on our knees like we did before. This time, let's ask God to shrink your income so you can afford to give only $1 a week."

What we give is not nearly as important as how we live, but the manner in which we live is often governed by how we give. If we're under grace, we should learn the art of joyful giving—not what we're required to give but what we're inspired to give.

During the reign of Alexander the Great, a beggar approached the emperor. He reached into a small bag and gave the beggar some gold coins. An aide to Alexander was startled by the generosity of the gift and said, "Sir, you've given this beggar gold coins when simple copper would have been sufficient." The emperor replied, "Copper would surely have suited the beggar's need, but gold suits Alexander's giving."

What we leave behind is more than money and possessions. We also leave behind a legacy that includes the spirit in which we gave.

Questions for Reflection and Discussion

1. What does the Bible teach about borrowing money and going into debt?

2. What is the most important reason for giving for a person of faith?

3. What does the author mean by "the art of joyful giving"?

4. Why are money and giving such sensitive, controversial subjects for most people?

5. In your opinion, why have state lotteries and legalized gambling become so popular in recent years?

6. Why is it important that we learn how to manage and protect our financial assets?

TWENTY-ONE

Rare, Medium, or Well-Done?

My favorite epitaph is the one that says, "I told you I was sick!" A few years ago, a journalism student working on a college newspaper was conducting an interview with me. She surprised me with her question: "What would you like inscribed on your tombstone?"

At the time I was asked the question, I had not yet turned forty. I was somewhat taken aback by that question, in fact. I don't remember exactly what I said in response, but I do remember fumbling about for an answer and attempting to mask my unease with thinking about something so terminal as my tombstone. Since that time, I've had a chance to think about a more thoughtful response to the question.

The kind of legacy we leave is tied directly to the kind of life we live. The fruit of the tree will always bear a genetic relationship to the root of the tree. A life that was lived selfishly and carelessly will not

> *A life that was lived selfishly and carelessly will not blossom forth into something dramatically different when it ends.*

blossom forth into something dramatically different when it ends. The kernel of corn produces corn. The tomato seed produces a tomato plant and more tomatoes. A grain of wheat has the capacity to produce only more wheat.

The life of a caring, loving, hardworking, generous person will leave a much different mark than that of a person who spoke ill of others, was manipulative, thoughtless, cruel, and hoarded everything he had. One thing is certain: When it comes to material things, we'll leave it all. There's no "carry forward" of property when it comes to the afterlife. The only treasure that can be sent ahead is the treasure of the soul.

In the end, it's not the amount of cash we have but the level of character we possess that determines how we will be remembered and how we'll live in the next life that God has prepared. There are three distinct possibilities.

Unprepared

Pity the person who spends a lifetime seeking to be famous and wealthy, achieves both goals, and in the end has nothing else to show for his life. It reminds us of the man Jesus spoke of in Luke 12:20.

He accummulated great wealth, but God said of him: "You fool! This very night your life will be demanded from you. Then who will get what you have prepared for yourself?"

There are many people whose lives revolve around stock splits, economic expansions, recessions, inflation numbers, and employment figures. But they're not prepared for the conclusion of life and the beginning of eternity.

Rising to the Highest Level of Mediocrity

Someone said that the person who seeks to travel in the middle of the road today will be roadkill tomorrow. On some things we can't be both for and against, hot and cold, up and down, north and south. We have to take a stand.

As we face the terminal nature of life, at some point we must decide whether we believe in God and where that belief will take us. We have to move past the notion that we can make everyone happy. We must get over the fact that we cannot accept all things as true. We cannot place our faith in the Jesus of the Bible and put our faith in the innate goodness of man at the same time.

> *We cannot place our faith in the Jesus of the Bible and put our faith in the innate goodness of man at the same time.*

It is sad to think of a person who lives life so unprepared that he ignores what happens when the curtain closes. It's equally sad when someone believes it's possible to accept everything, believe everything, and embrace everything that has been put forth about the ultimate destination of the human spirit. If God did become a person, lived on earth in the form of Jesus, died as he died, rose from the grave to conquer death, and invited us to share eternal life with him, that will be proved at death.

I can't say with personal authority what will happen to a person who travels the path I've chosen. I only must be certain the path I've chosen will lead me to a life beyond that corresponds to a life below.

It's tempting to try living in such a way that we offend no one and please everyone. But the person going down the center line only meets oncoming traffic.

Fully Cooked

I've thought a lot in recent years about what I hope will be said of me and carved into stone once my physical body turns to dust while my spirit soars to God. In speeches I often say, "I've learned not to live for the weekend or the next event or the next election but rather to live for the next lifetime."

If at the conclusion of my tenure on earth I could hear six words uttered by my Creator, I would feel I had crossed the finish line, breaking the tape with my chest and achieving the championship. These six words can shape our decisions, guide our activities, and help us establish our priorities. These six words can change our relationship to God and our relationships with others.

More than I hope to have kind words written about me in the newspaper or to be mentioned as a footnote in our state's history, I hope that when my life's journey is over I'll hear these six words: "Well done, good and faithful servant!" (Matt. 25:23).

> *I hope that when my life's journey is over I'll hear these six words: "Well done, good and faithful servant" (Matt. 25:23).*

That's it. That's what I want to hear—six words worth living for and dying for. Rather than being noted for some singular earthly achievement, I would rather the totality of my life be evaluated. I hope not to be seen as some raw and unprepared dish that held great promise but was never fully cooked. Neither do I want my life to be something that appears finished on the outside but inside is still raw from never having the core inner values brought to maturity.

I would hope my life would be full and complete. I would hope it could be said of me, "Well done, good and faithful servant!" (Matt. 25:23).

Questions for Reflection and Discussion

1. Have you thought about the epitaph that you would like inscribed on your tombstone? What features of your life will likely be remembered after you are gone?

2. What does the author mean by this statement: "The only treasure that can be sent ahead is the treasure of the soul"?

3. How should a person get prepared for the conclusion of life and the beginning of eternity?

4. What actions and behaviors are you demonstrating today that are leading toward this ultimate evaluation by the Master: "Well done, good and faithful servant!" (Matt. 25:23)?

"Keep Your Fork!"

A woman had been diagnosed with a terminal illness, She had been given three months to live. As she was getting her things in order, she discussed her final wishes with her pastor. She told him the songs she wanted sung at her funeral, the Scriptures she wanted him to read, and the outfit she wanted to be buried in. The woman also asked to be buried with her favorite Bible.

As the pastor was preparing to leave, the woman remembered something very important to her.

"There's one more thing," she said excitedly.

"What's that?" came the pastor's reply.

"This is very important," the woman continued. "I want to be buried with a fork in my right hand."

The pastor stood looking at the woman, not knowing quite what to say.

"That surprises you, doesn't it?" the woman asked.

"Well, to be honest, I'm puzzled by your request," said the pastor.

The woman explained. "In all my years of attending church socials and potluck dinners, I always remember that when the dishes of the main course were being cleared, someone would inevitably lean over and say, 'Keep your fork.'

"It was my favorite part because I knew that something better was coming—like velvety chocolate cake or deep-dish apple pie. Something wonderful, and with substance!

"So I just want people to see me there in that casket with a fork in my hand, and I want them to wonder, *What's with the fork?* Then I want you to tell them, 'Keep your fork! The best is yet to come!'"

The pastor's eyes welled up with tears of joy as he hugged the woman good-bye. He knew this would be one of the last times he would see her before her death. But he also knew that the woman had a better grasp of heaven than he did. She knew that something better was coming.

At the funeral people were walking by the woman's casket, and they saw the pretty dress she was wearing and her favorite Bible and the fork placed in her right hand. Over and over the pastor heard the question, "What's with the fork?" And over and over he smiled.

During his message, the pastor told the people of the conversation he had with the woman shortly before she died. He also told them about the fork and about what it symbolized to her. The pastor told the people how he could not stop thinking about the fork and told them that they probably would not be able to stop thinking about it either. He was right.

So the next time you reach down for your fork, let it remind you—oh so gently—that the best is yet to come.